Anticipation

By Heidi Pridemore

Finished Size: 58" x 70" (147 cm x 178 cm)
Pattern Level: Advanced beginner
All seam allowances are ¼".
Please read all directions before beginning and press carefully step-by-step

You will be using fourteen different color fabrics in the blocks. It is very helpful to cut a color swatch of each fabric and create a color key using this chart to keep track of each fabric.

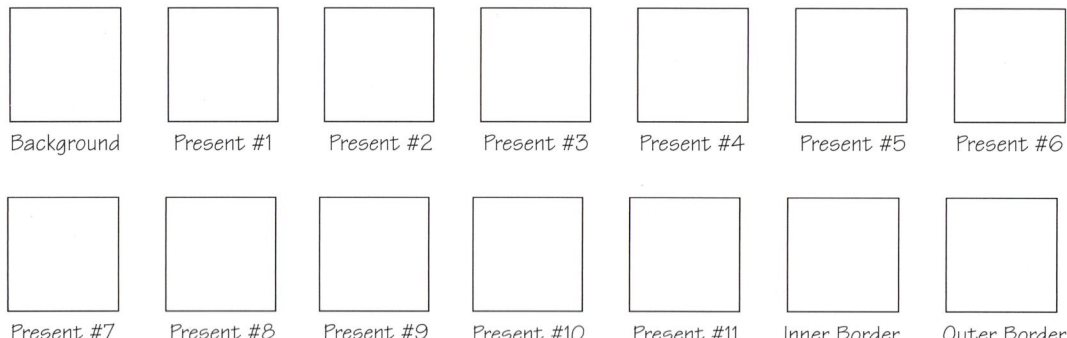

CUTTING OUT THE PIECES

All measurements include a ¼" seam allowance. Follow **Rotary Cutting**, page 68, to cut fabric. Cutting lengths for borders are exact. Refer to **Template Cutting**, page 69, to make template from Template A pattern, page 9.

BLOCK ONE
From red print (background) fabric, cut:
- Six 2½" x 4½" rectangles
- Three 1½" x 4½" rectangles
- Six 1½" x 6½" rectangles

From the green swirl (present #1) fabric, cut:
- Three 4½" squares

From purple print (present #2) fabric, cut:
- Three 6½" squares

From yellow stripe (present #3) fabric, cut:
- Three 4½" x 9½" rectangles

BLOCK TWO
From red print (background) fabric, cut:
- Four 2½" x 4½" rectangles
- Twelve Template A
- Two 2½" squares
- Two 2½" x 6½" rectangles

From blue dot (present #4) fabric, cut:
- Twelve Template A
- Four 2½" x 4½" rectangles

From yellow print (present #5) fabric, cut:
- Two 4½" x 6½" rectangles

From green print (present #6) fabric, cut:
- Two 6½" x 8½" rectangles

BLOCK TWO REVERSED
From red print (background) fabric, cut:
- Two 2½" x 4½" rectangles
- Six Template A reversed
- One 2½" square
- One 2½" x 6½" rectangle

From blue dot (present #4) fabric, cut:
- Six Template A reversed
- Two 2½" x 4½" rectangles

From yellow print (present #5) fabric, cut:
- One 4½" x 6½" rectangle

From green print (present #6) fabric, cut:
- One 6½" x 8½" rectangle

BLOCK THREE

From red print (background) fabric, cut:
- Four 2½" x 10½" rectangles

From purple star (present #7) fabric, cut:
- Two 8½" x 10½" rectangles

BLOCK FOUR

From red print (background) fabric, cut:
- Six 1½" x 6½" rectangles

From black dot (present #8) fabric, cut:
- Four 6½" x 11½" rectangles

From yellow print (present #5) fabric, cut:
- One 6½" x 11½" rectangle

From purple star (present #7) fabric, cut:
- One 6½" x 11½" rectangle

BLOCK FIVE

From red print (background) fabric, cut:
- Three 4½" x 8½" rectangles
- Three 1½" x 8½" rectangles

From green stars (present #9) fabric, cut:
- Three 7½" x 8½" rectangles

BLOCK SIX

From red print (background) fabric, cut:
- One 2½" x 4½" rectangle
- One 2½" x 10½" rectangle
- One 4½" x 5½" rectangle
- One 1½" x 10½" rectangle

From purple dot (present #10) fabric, cut:
- One 4½" x 8½" rectangle

From blue star (present #11) fabric, cut:
- One 5½" x 6½" rectangle

SASHING AND BORDERS

From red print (background) fabric, cut:
- Four 3" x 56½" sashing strips, pieced as necessary.
- One 3" x 46½" top sashing strip, pieced as necessary.

From the blue speckle (inner border) fabric, cut:
- Two 2" x 59" inner side borders, pieced as necessary.
- Two 2" x 49½" inner top/bottom borders, pieced as necessary.

From the multi stripe (outer border) fabric, cut:
- Two lengthwise 4½" x 62" outer side borders
- Two lengthwise 4½" x 57½" outer top/bottom borders

From the binding fabric, cut:
- Seven 2¼" strips.

MAKING THE BLOCKS

Follow **Piecing** and **Pressing**, page 69, to make blocks.

ATTACH THE RIBBONS TO THE PACKAGES

1. After cutting the fabric for the presents listed for each block, cut a piece of ribbon at least 1" longer than the fabric square or rectangle.
2. Place fusible tape on the back of each ribbon piece.
3. Refer to photo to place ribbon; iron in place. When sewing the blocks together, be sure to catch the ribbon ends in the seams.

BLOCK ONE

Refer to **Fig. 1** to lay out the pieces of the block and sew them into three sections. Join the sections to complete the block. Make three of Block One.

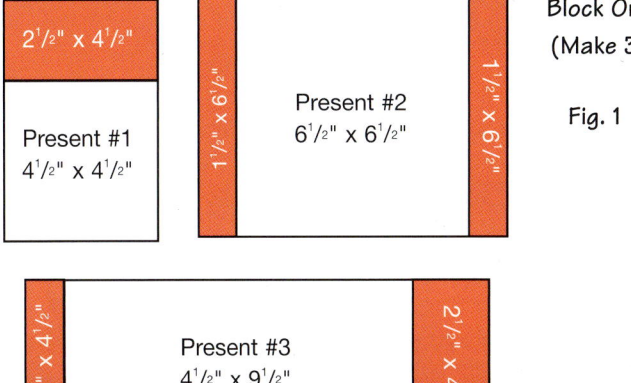

Block One (Make 3)

Fig. 1

BLOCK TWO

Sew a background Template A to a present #4 Template A to make a pieced rectangle **(Fig. 2)**. Make six rectangles. Refer to **Fig. 3** to lay out the pieces for one Block Two. Sew them into four sections as shown. Join the sections to complete the blocks. Make two of Block Two.

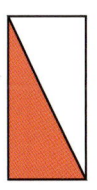

Fig. 2

Block Two
(Make 2)

Fig. 3

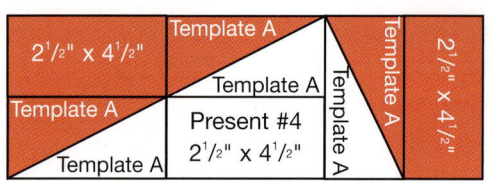
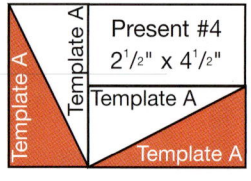
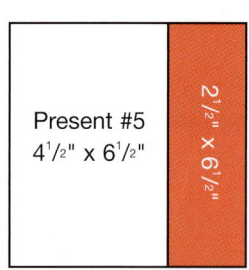
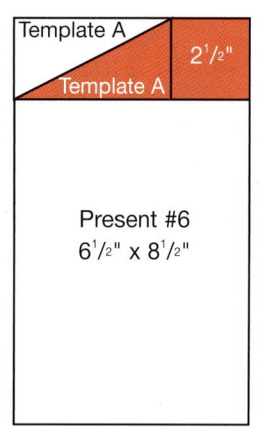

BLOCK THREE

Sew the 2½" x 10½" background rectangles to the long sides of the present rectangle to complete the block **(Fig. 6)**. Make two of Block Three.

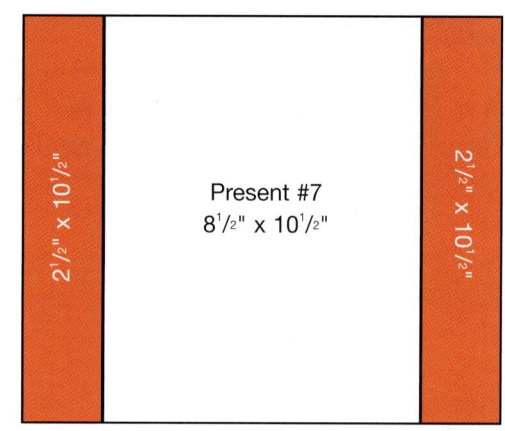

Block Three
(Make 2)

Fig. 6

BLOCK TWO REVERSED

Sew a background Template A Reversed to a present #4 Template A Reversed to make a pieced rectangle. Make six rectangles **(Fig. 4)**. Refer to **Fig. 5** to lay out the pieces for one Block Two Reversed. Sew them into four sections as shown. Join the sections to complete the block. Make one of Block Two Reversed.

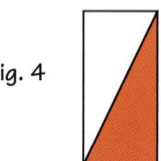

Fig. 4

BLOCK FOUR

Sew the 1½" x 6½" background rectangle to the right side of the present #5, present #7 and present #8 rectangles **(Fig. 7)**. Make six total of Block Four.

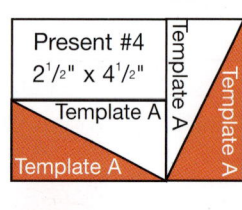

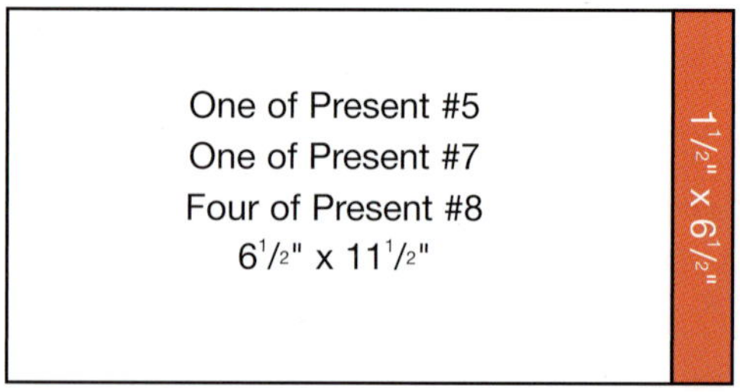

Block Four
(Make 6)

Fig. 7

Block Two
Reversed
(Make 1)

Fig. 5

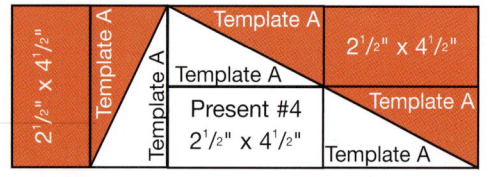
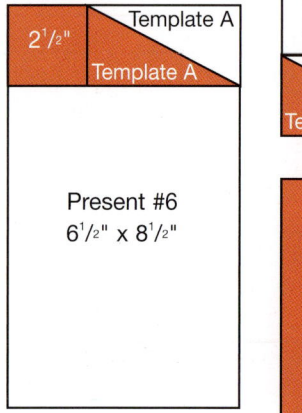

BLOCK FIVE

Sew the 1½" x 8½" rectangle to the right side of the package rectangle. Sew the 4½" x 8½" strip to the left side to complete a block **(Fig. 8)**. Make three of Block Five.

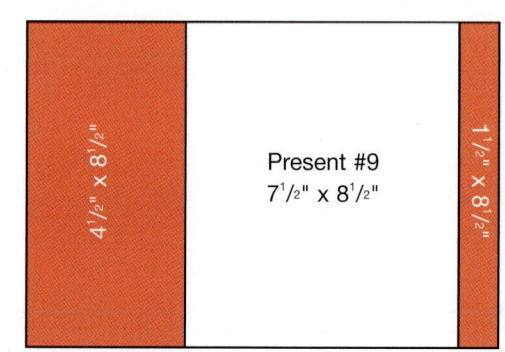

Block Five
(Make 3)

Fig. 8

BLOCK SIX

Refer to **Fig. 9** to Lay out all the pieces for the block and sew them into sections as shown. Join the sections to complete the block. Make one of Block Six.

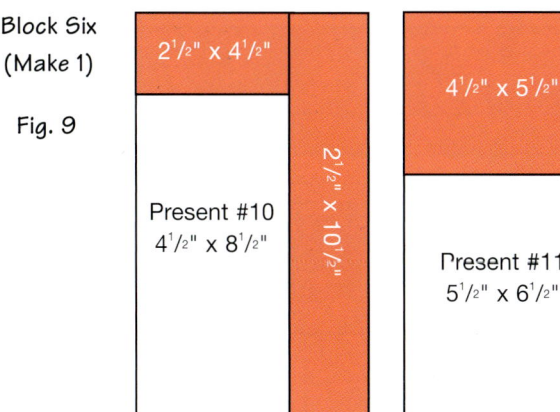

Block Six (Make 1)

Fig. 9

ASSEMBLING THE QUILT TOP

Refer to photo and the **Quilt Top Diagram** for block placement. To sew borders and sashings to Quilt Top Center, match centers and corners and ease in fullness.

1. Lay out the blocks in three vertical rows. Sew the blocks into rows.
2. Add two side sashing strips between the rows and to each side of the rows. Add the top sashing strip to the center.
3. Add the inner side borders to the center, then the inner top and bottom borders.
4. Add the outer side borders to the center, then the outer top and bottom borders.

COMPLETING THE QUILT

1. Follow **Quilting**, page 71, to mark, layer, and quilt as desired.
2. Follow **Making Straight Grain Binding**, page 73, and **Attaching Binding with Mitered Corners**, page 73, to attach binding to quilt.
3. Referring to photo for placement, make bows from remaining ribbon and hand stitch or pin them to the finished quilt.

Note: for a washable quilt, hem the unfinished edges of the ribbons and attach the bows with safety pins. Hand-wash the ribbons and line dry.

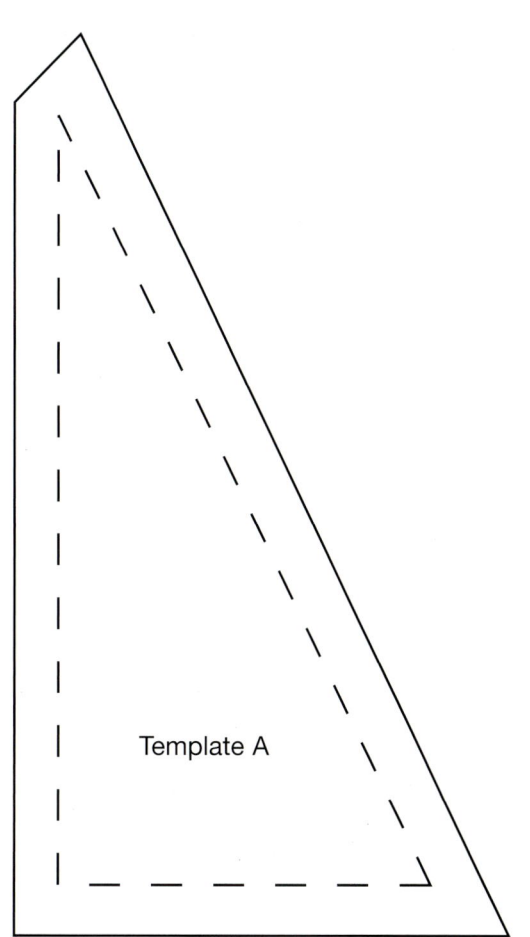

Template A

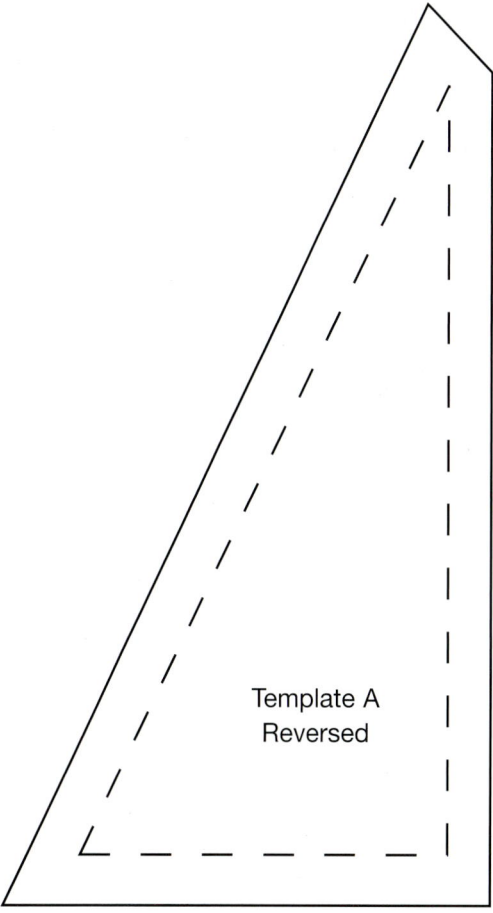

Template A Reversed

Quilt Top Diagram

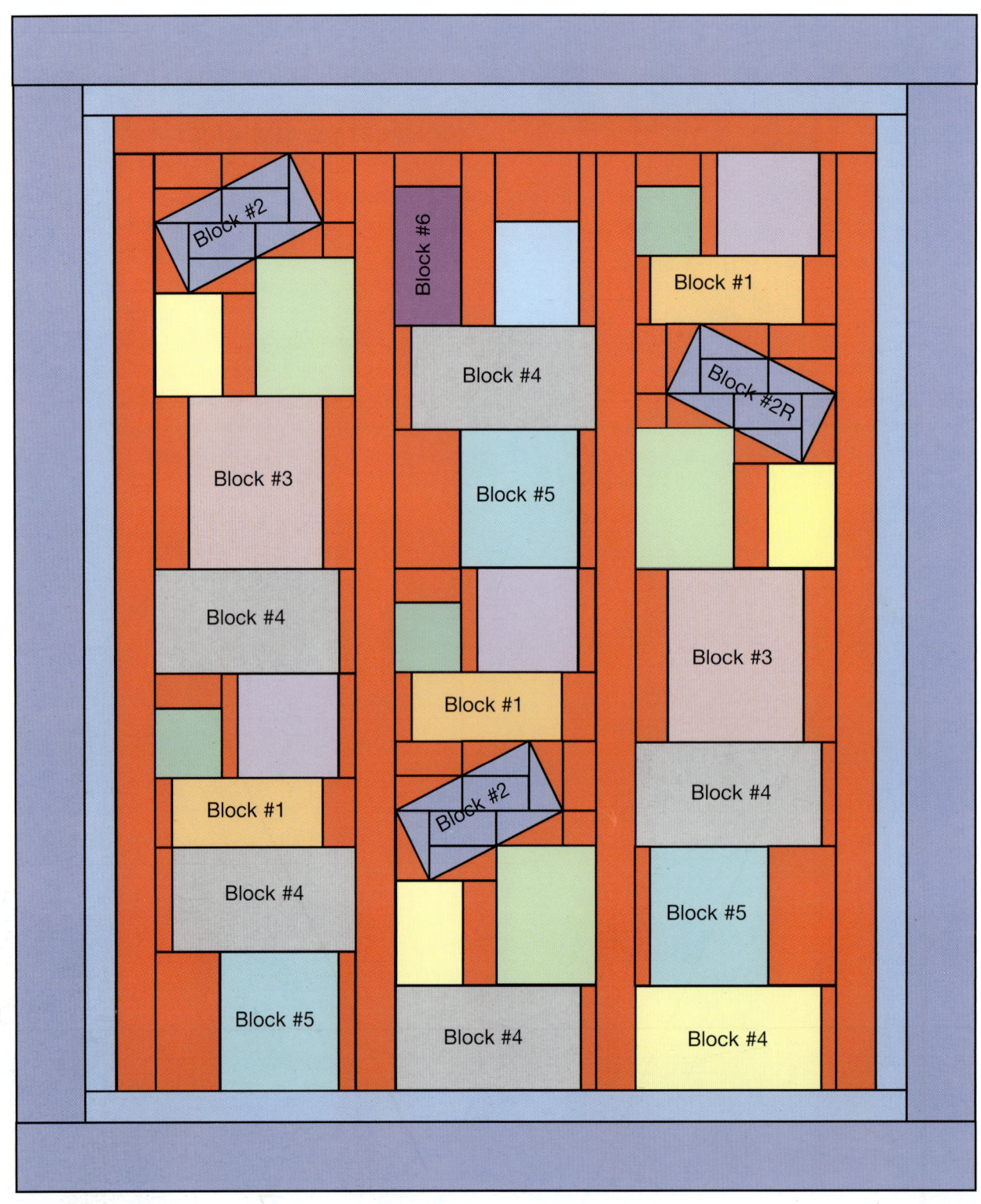

Cup of Joe

Supplies Needed:

FABRIC:

1 yd. (.91 m)	Background - White
¾ yd. (69 cm)	Sashing, Checkerboard & Flying Geese - Black
¼ yd. (23 cm) each	Coffee Mugs - Green, Pink, Orange, Red, Purple, Yellow, & Blue
¼ yd. (23 cm)	Coffee Pot - Multi-Color Print #1
⅜ yd. (34 cm)	Checkerboard & Binding - Rainbow Print
⅜ yd. (34 cm)	Flying Geese Border - Multi-Color Print #2
¼ yd. (23 cm)	Coffee - Tan
1¼ yd. (1.1 m)	Backing Fabric

Other Supplies:

1 ½ yds. (1.37 m) Paper-backed Fusible Web
Stabilizer
Appliqué Pressing Sheet
40" (102 cm) Square of Batting

Cup of Joe

By Heidi Pridemore

Finished Size: 34" square
Pattern Level: Beginner
All seam allowances are 1/4".
Please read all directions before beginning and press carefully step-by-step.

Note: This Pattern has been written to use the fusible web appliqué technique. I recommend using an appliqué pressing sheet for easier assembly.

CUTTING OUT THE PIECES

Follow **Rotary Cutting**, page 68, to cut fabric. Refer to **Preparing Fusible Appliqué Pieces**, page 70, to use patterns, pages 16-21.

From white, cut:
- One 11" square (coffee pot background)
- Twelve 6 3/4" squares (mug backgrounds)

From black, cut:
- Twelve 1 1/2" x 6 3/4" strips (sashing)
- Two 1 1/2" x 14" strips (first border)
- Two 1 1/2" x 16" strips (first border)
- Two 1 1/2" x 28 1/2" strips (second border)
- Two 1 1/2" x 30 1/2" strips (second border)
- 100 2" squares (checkerboard, Flying Geese corners)

From multi-print #2, cut:
- 40 rectangles, 2" x 3 1/2" (Flying Geese centers)

From rainbow print, cut:
- Sixteen 2" squares (checkerboard)
- Four 2 1/4" strips (binding)

TO CUT OUT THE APPLIQUÉS:

1. Trace the patterns for the coffee pot and coffee mugs on the paper side of fusible web with a permanent marker or pencil, following the manufacturer's instructions.
2. Roughly cut out each shape from the fusible web.
3. Using the quilt photo and the fabrics listed on the patterns as guides, iron each shape on the back of the appropriate color fabric.
4. Cut out each shape on the traced lines.

ASSEMBLING THE QUILT TOP

Follow **Piecing** and **Pressing**, page 69, to make the blocks. Follow **Satin Stitch Appliqué**, page 70, to add appliqués.

COFFEE MUG & COFFEE POT SQUARES:

1. Place the appliqué pressing sheet over the Mug #1 assembly diagram and arrange the pieces. Press and remove Mug #1. Repeat for each mug and the coffee pot.
2. Using the quilt **Quilt Top Diagram** as a guide, tilt each mug in the indicated direction and iron on a 6 3/4" white square.
3. Iron the coffee pot on the 11" white square.
4. Finish the edges of the coffee mugs and coffee pot with a decorative stitch such as a button hole or satin stitch.

CHECKERBOARD BORDERS:

1. Starting with a black square and alternating four 2" black squares and three 2" rainbow squares, sew the squares together to create one side checkerboard border.
2. Repeat to make a second side checkerboard border.
3. Sew one side of the checkerboard border to each side of the coffee pot square.

4. Starting with a rainbow square and alternating five 2" rainbow squares and four 2" black squares, sew the squares together to create the top checkerboard border.
5. Repeat to make the bottom checkerboard border.
6. Sew the top and bottom checkerboard borders to the coffee pot square. This completes the quilt center.
7. Sew one 1½" x 14" black strip to each side of the quilt center.
8. Sew one 1½" x 16" black strip to the top and bottom of the quilt center.

COFFEE MUGS:
1. Using the **Quilt Top Diagram** as a guide for placement, lay out the coffee mugs with the sashing to form the two side rows and the top and bottom rows.
2. Sew each row together and press.
3. Sew the side rows to the quilt center.
4. Sew the top and bottom rows to the quilt center.

SECOND BORDER:
1. Sew one 1½" x 28½" second border strip to each side of the quilt top.
2. Sew one 1½" x 30½" second border to the top and another to the bottom of the quilt top.

FLYING GEESE OUTER BORDER:
1. Place one 2" black square on the top left side of one 2" x 3½" multi-color print #2 rectangle, right sides together. Mark and sew across the diagonal from the upper right corner to the lower left corner. **(Fig. 1)**

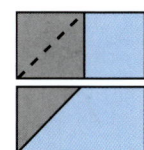

Fig. 1

2. Open out the triangle formed and finger press the seam open. Check that the corners are aligned squarely. Flip the triangle back down and trim away the excess fabric, leaving a ¼" seam allowance.
3. Place another 2" black square on the top right side of the same 2" x 3½" rectangle, right sides together. Mark and sew across the diagonal from the upper left corner to the lower right corner. **(Fig. 2)**

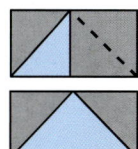

Fig. 2

4. Open out the triangle formed and finger press the seam open. Check that the corners are aligned squarely. Flip the triangle back down and trim away the excess fabric, leaving a ¼" seam allowance.
5. Repeat Steps 1 - 4 to make 40 Flying Geese units in all.
6. Sew ten Flying Geese units together, short side to short side, with the multi-color print triangles all pointing in the same direction. **(Fig. 3)** This will make one outer border.

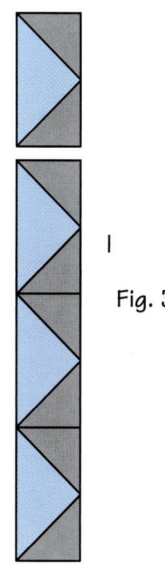

Fig. 3

7. Repeat Step 6 to make four outer borders in all.
8. Sew one Flying Geese outer border to each side of the quilt top with the multi-color print triangles pointing out.
9. Sew one 2" black square to each end of one of the outer borders to make the top outer border.
10. Repeat Step 9 to make the bottom outer border.
11. Sew the top and bottom outer borders to the quilt top.

COMPLETING THE QUILT
1. Follow **Quilting**, page 71, to mark, layer, and quilt as desired. The quilt in the photo was quilted with stitch-in-the-ditch around the blocks and through the rows and borders. Loose stippling was added in the white background around the coffee mugs and coffee pot.

2. Follow **Making Straight Grain Binding**, page 73, and **Attaching Binding with Mitered Corners**, page 73, to attach binding to quilt.

Mug #1 Assembly Drawing

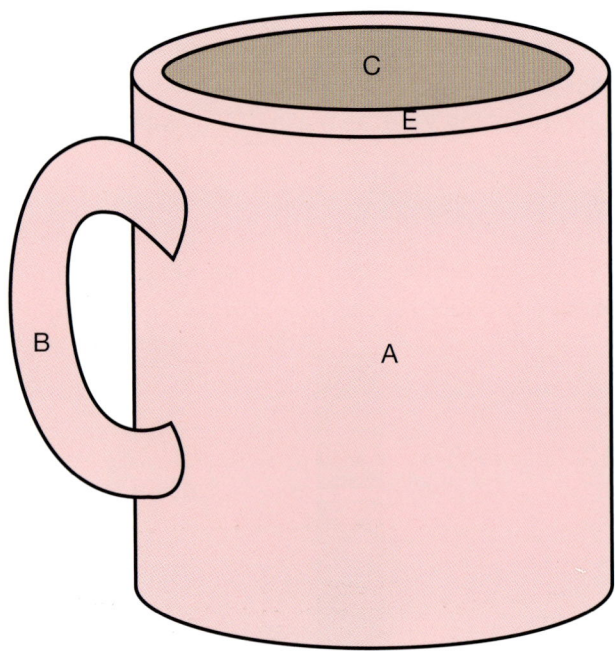

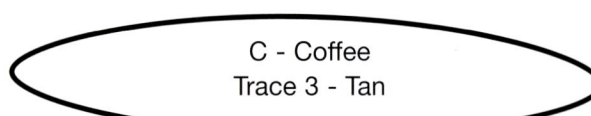

C - Coffee
Trace 3 - Tan

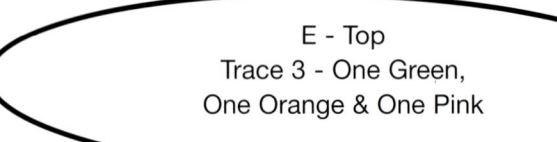

E - Top
Trace 3 - One Green,
One Orange & One Pink

Mug #1 Patterns

Patterns are reversed for fusible appliqué

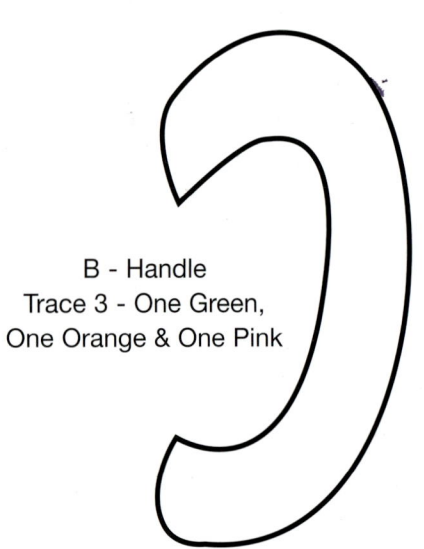

B - Handle
Trace 3 - One Green,
One Orange & One Pink

A - Cup
Trace 3 - One Green,
One Orange & One Pink

Mug #2 Assembly Drawing

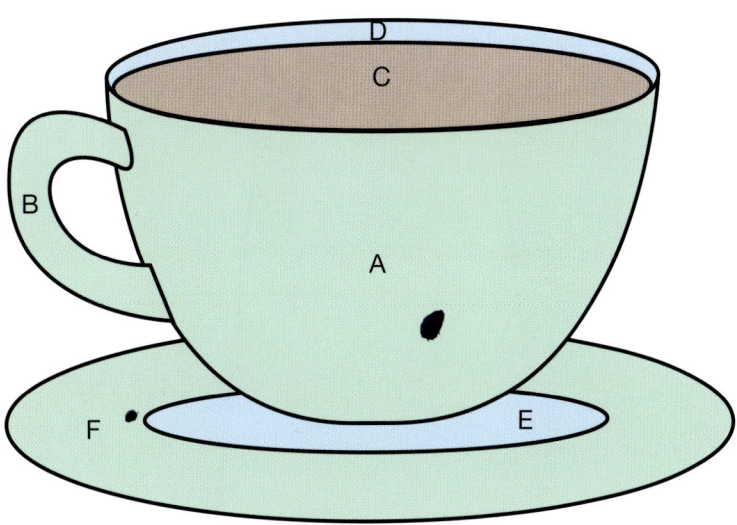

Mug #2 Patterns

Patterns are reversed for fusible appliqué

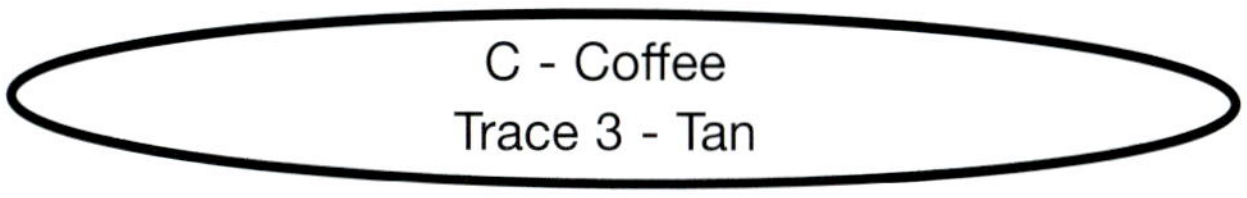

C - Coffee
Trace 3 - Tan

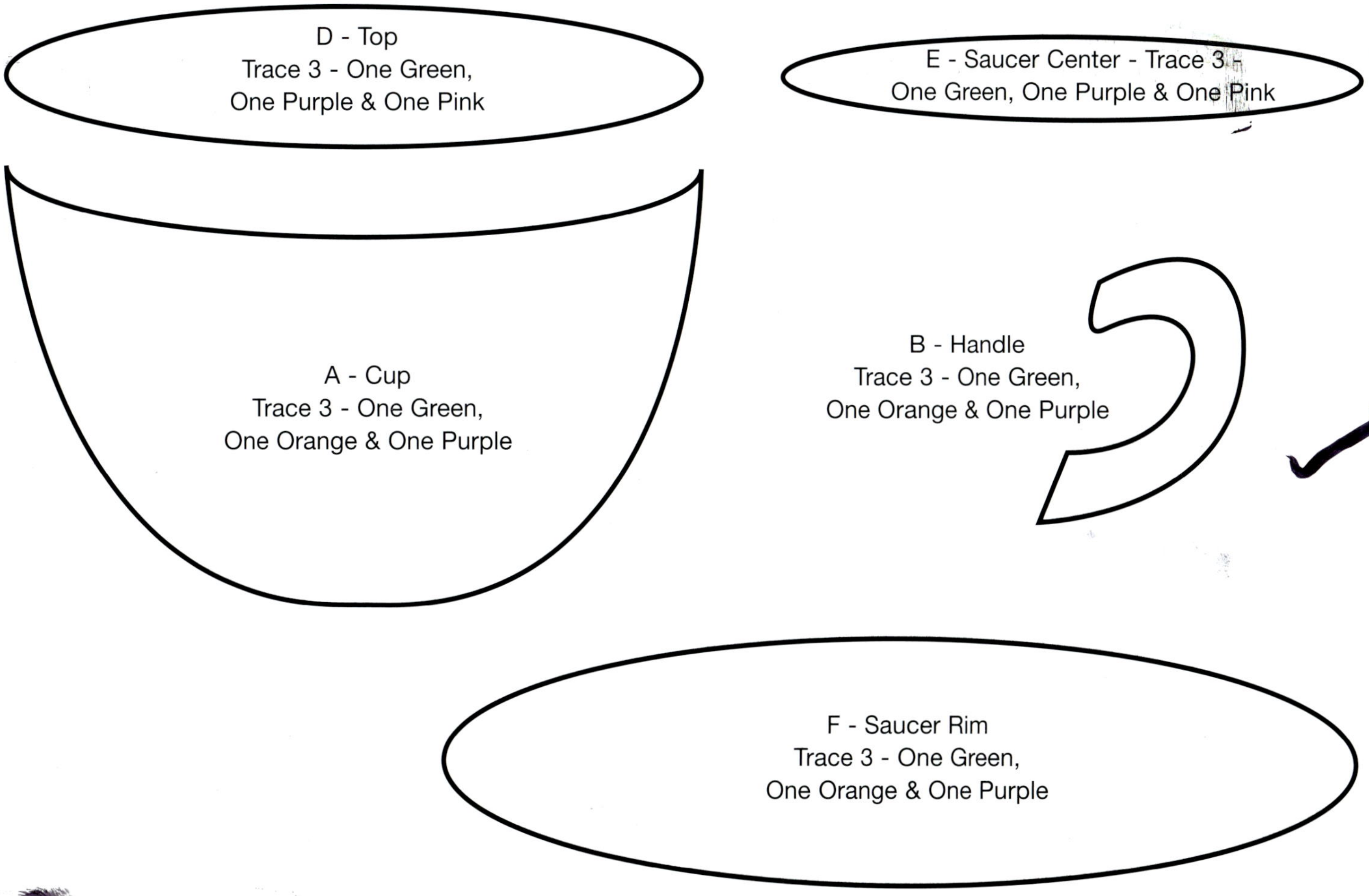

D - Top
Trace 3 - One Green,
One Purple & One Pink

E - Saucer Center - Trace 3 -
One Green, One Purple & One Pink

A - Cup
Trace 3 - One Green,
One Orange & One Purple

B - Handle
Trace 3 - One Green,
One Orange & One Purple

F - Saucer Rim
Trace 3 - One Green,
One Orange & One Purple

Mug #3 Assembly Drawing

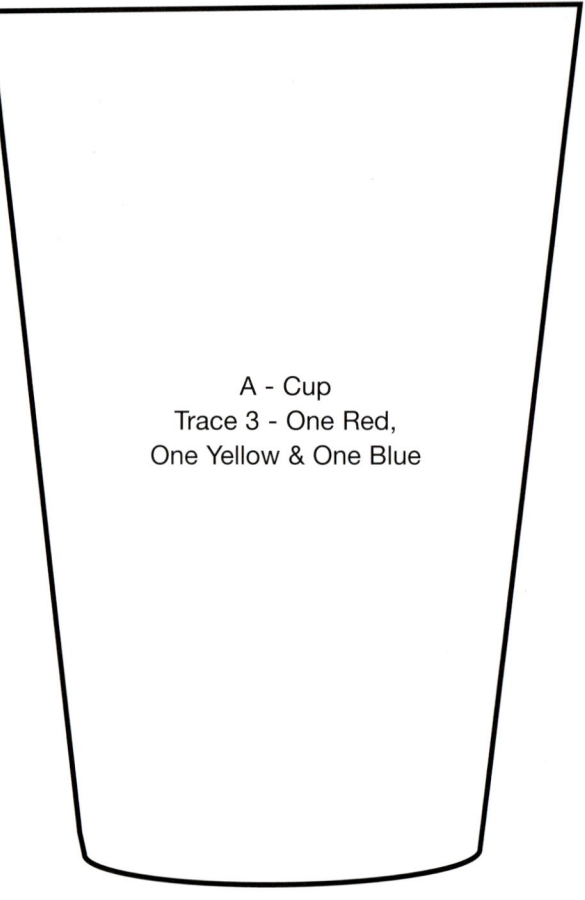

A - Cup
Trace 3 - One Red,
One Yellow & One Blue

Mug #3 Patterns

Patterns are reversed for fusible appliqué

B - Coffee - Trace 3 - Tan

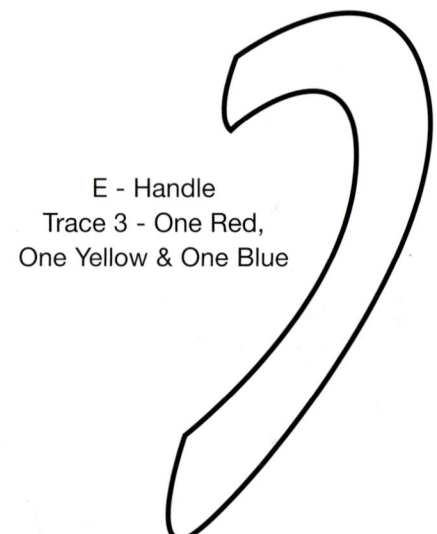

E - Handle
Trace 3 - One Red,
One Yellow & One Blue

C - Top
Trace 3 - One Red,
One Yellow & One Blue

Mug #4 Assembly Drawing

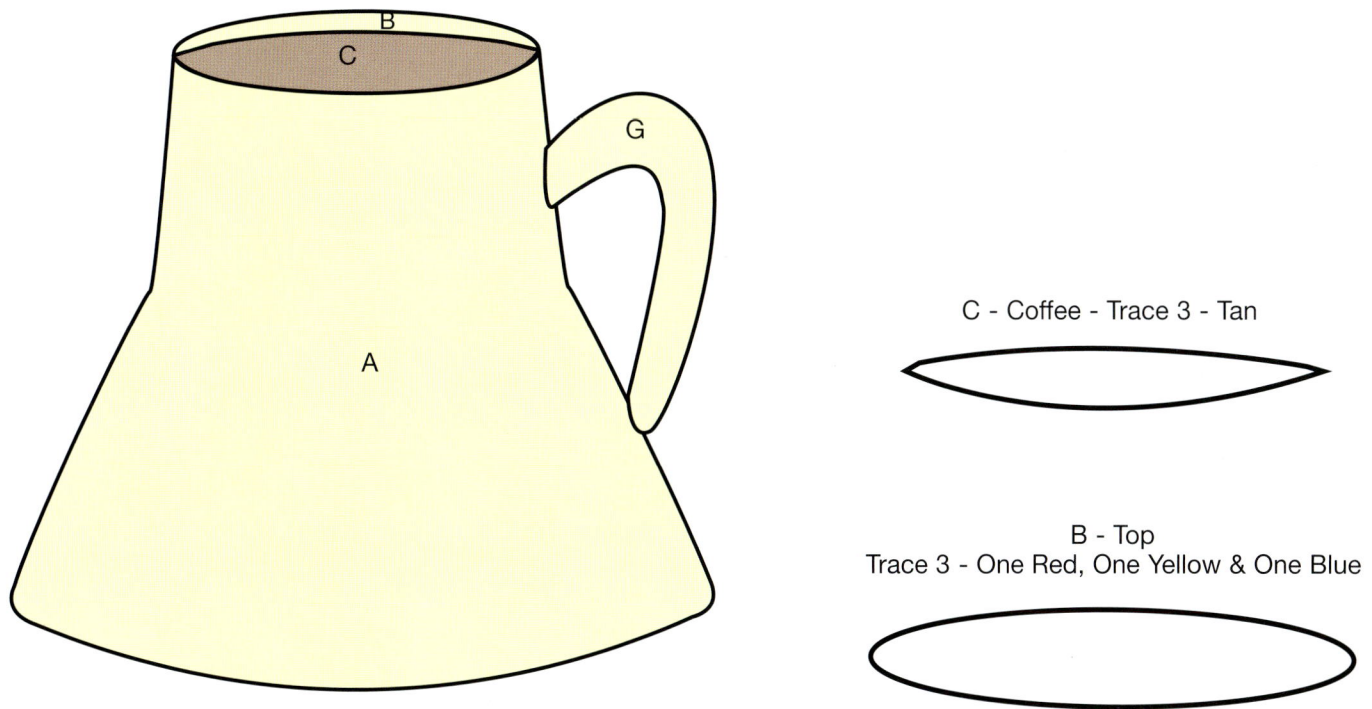

C - Coffee - Trace 3 - Tan

B - Top
Trace 3 - One Red, One Yellow & One Blue

Mug #4 Patterns

Patterns are reversed for fusible appliqué

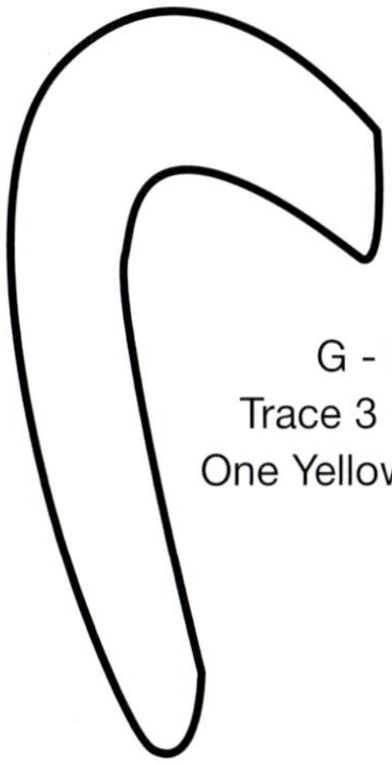

G - Handle
Trace 3 - One Red,
One Yellow & One Blue

A - Cup
Trace 3 - One Red,
One Yellow & One Blue

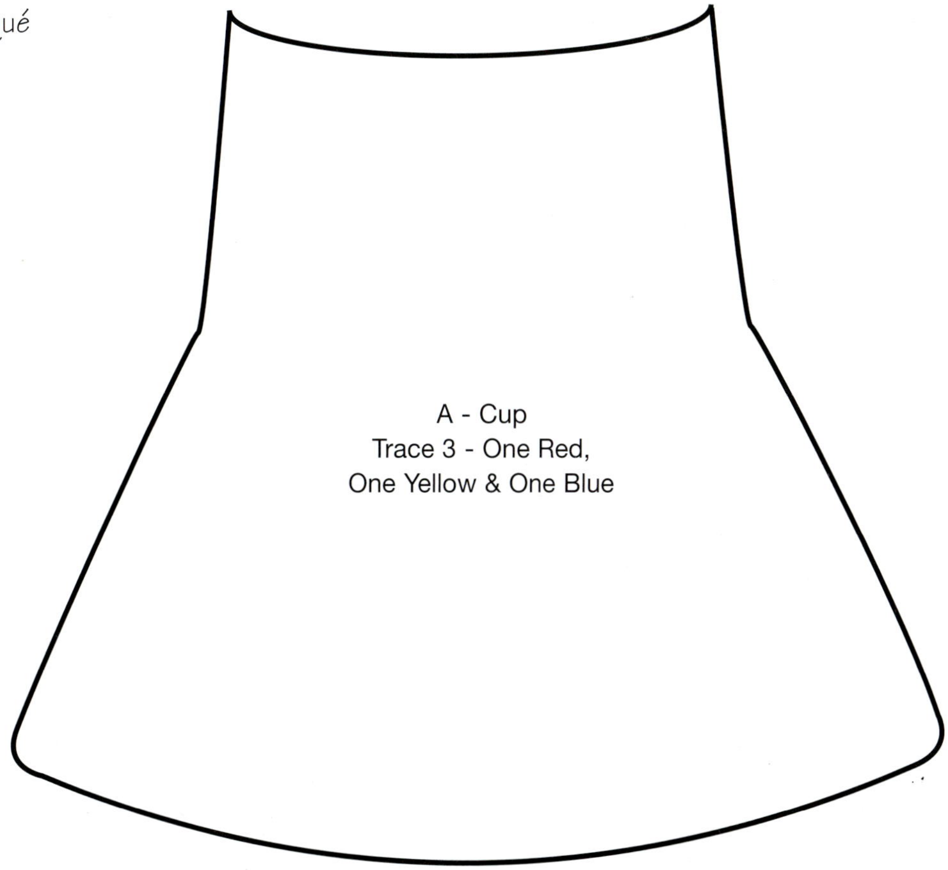

Coffee Pot Assembly Drawing

D
C
B
H
F
E
A
G

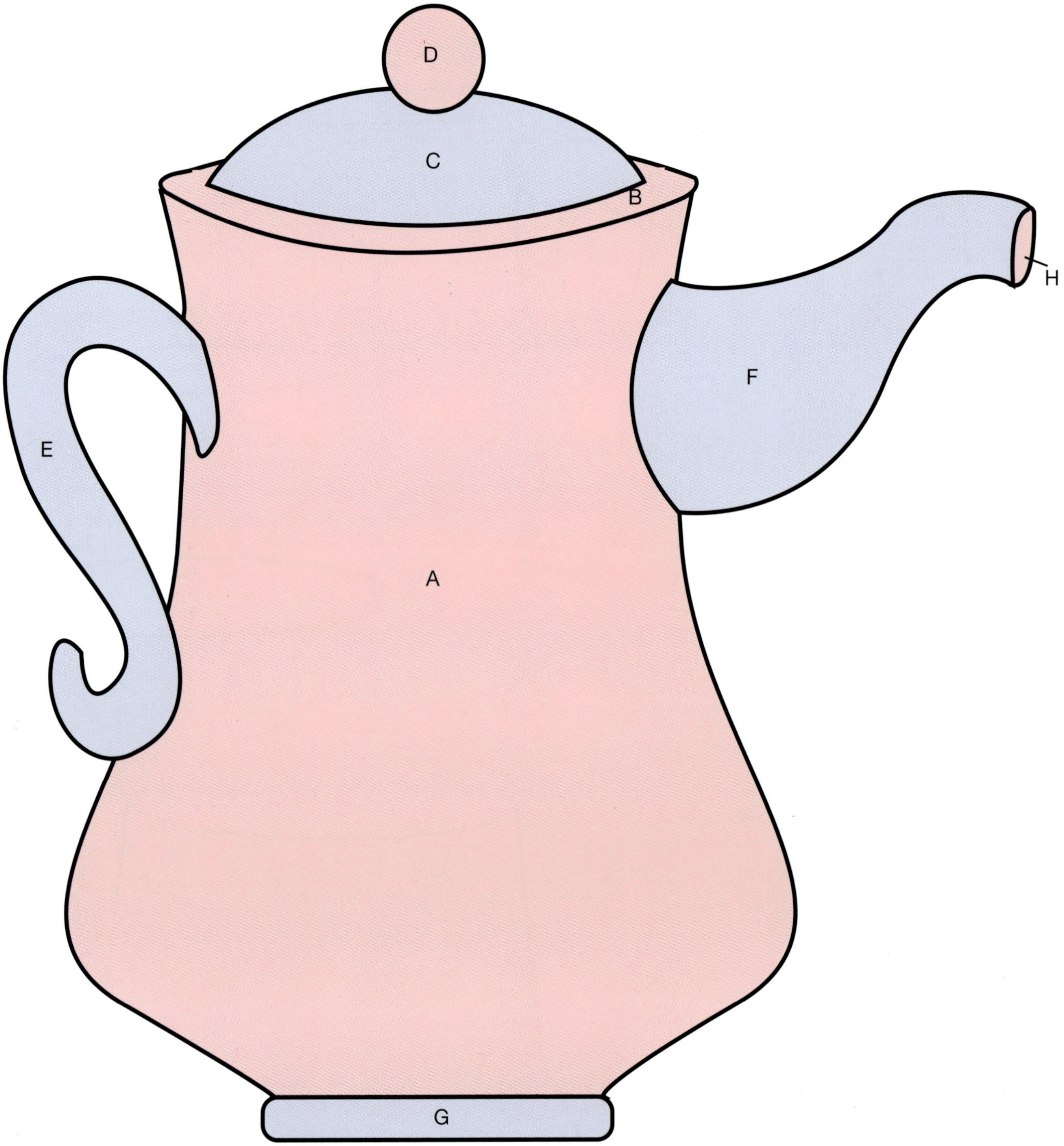

Coffee Pot Patterns

Patterns are reversed for fusible appliqué

E - Handle
Trace 1 - Pink

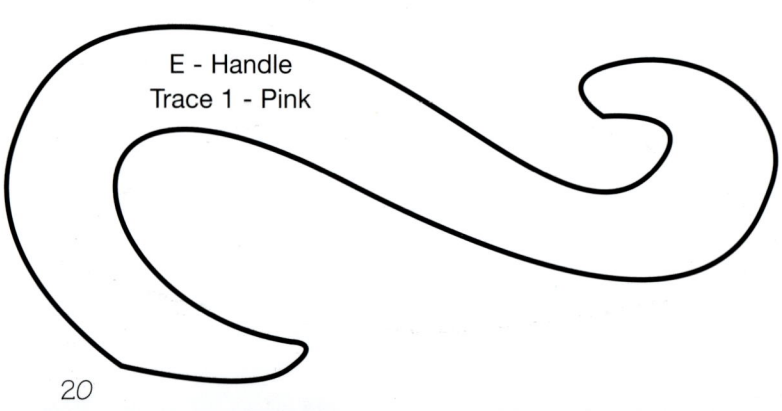

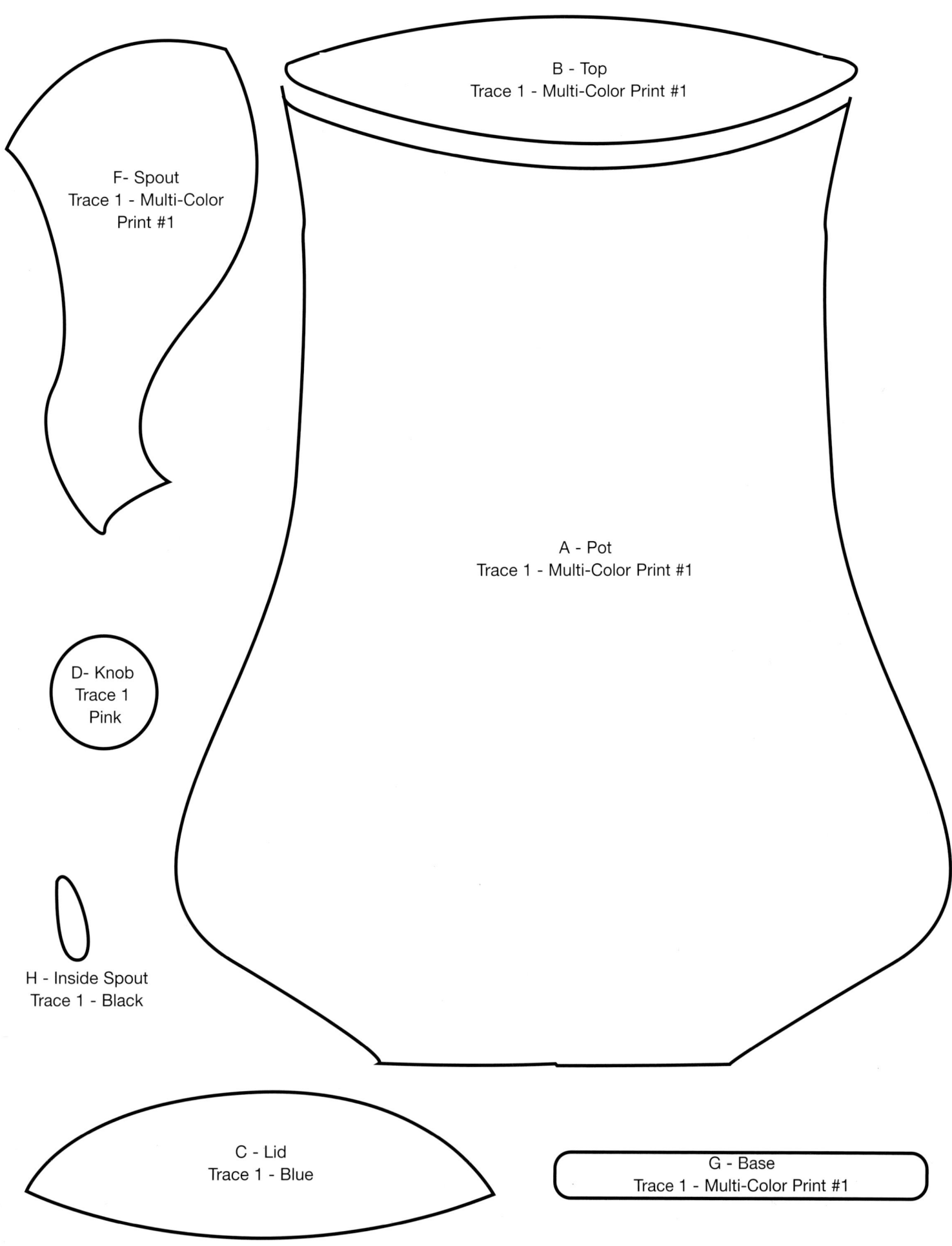

Quilt Top Diagram

Out to Lunch

Supplies Needed:

FABRIC:

2¼ yds. (2.1 m)	Background Fabric (non directional) - Bright Pink
⅝ yd. (57 cm)	2 Frogs - Light Bright Green
⅝ yd. (57 cm)	2 Frogs - Meduim Bright Green
⅝ yd. (57 cm)	2 Frogs - Deep Bright Green
¼ yd. (23 cm)	Frogs' Eyes - White
⅛ yd. (12 cm)	Frogs' Eyeballs and Noses - Black
⅛ yd. (12 cm)	Frogs' Tongues - Hot Pink
1 yd. (.91 m)	Dragonfly Bodies & 1st Inner Border - Bright Blue
1½ yds. (1.4 m)	Dragonfly Wings - Black & White Narrow Striped
⅝ yd. (57 cm)	Second Inner Border - Lime Green
1½ yds. (1.4 m)	Outer Border & Binding - Bright Purple Print
4½ yds. (4.1 m)	Backing Fabric

Other Supplies:

¾ yd. (68 cm) Paper-backed Fusible Web

Stabilizer

63" x 77" (160 cm x 196 cm) Rectangle of Batting

Template Plastic

100 Small Safety Pins

Bright Blue Embroidery Floss

Out to Lunch

By Heidi Pridemore

Finished Size: 56" x 70" (142 cm x 178 cm)
Pattern Level: Advanced Beginner
All seam allowances are $1/4$".
Please read all directions before beginning and press carefully step-by-step.

CUTTING OUT THE PIECES:

Measurements include a $1/4$" seam allowance. Follow **Rotary Cutting**, page 68, to cut fabrics. Refer to **Template Cutting**, page 69, to make templates from the patterns for the dragonfly wings, page 32. Refer to **Preparing Fusible Appliqués**, page 70, to use dragonfly body pattern, page 32.

DRAGONFLY BACKGROUNDS:
From the background fabric, cut:
- Six $14^1/2$" squares

FROG BLOCKS
These cutting instructions are for one block. The number in parentheses is the number of pieces needed for all six blocks. For the frog bodies, cut two sets of each square in each of the three bright green fabrics to make six frogs in all.

From the (non-directional) background fabric, cut:
- Eighteen $1^1/2$" squares (108 total)
- Two $2^1/2$" x $9^1/2$" pieces (12 total)
- One $2^1/2$" x $10^1/2$" piece (6 total)
- One $2^1/2$" square (6 total)
- Two $1^1/2$" x $2^1/2$" pieces (12 total)

From white fabric, cut:
- Two $1^1/2$" x $3^1/2$" pieces (12 total)
- Four $1^1/2$" squares (24 total)

From black fabric, cut:
- Four $1^1/2$" squares (24 total)

From hot pink fabric, cut:
- Two $1^1/2$" x $3^1/2$" rectangles (12 total)

From the frog fabrics, cut two sets from *each* bright green:
- Three $1^1/2$" x $3^1/2$" rectangles
- Three $2^1/2$" squares
- Eight $1^1/2$" squares
- One $2^1/2$" x $10^1/2$" rectangle
- One $1^1/2$" x $4^1/2$" rectangle
- One $1^1/2$" x $6^1/2$" rectangle
- One $1^1/2$" x $5^1/2$" rectangle
- One $3^1/2$" x $14^1/2$"" rectangle
- Two $1^1/2$" x $7^1/2$" rectangles
- Two $1^1/2$" x $2^1/2$" rectangles

From the bright blue fabric, cut the dragonfly bodies:
1. Trace the Dragonfly pattern on the paper side of the fusible web. Roughly cut out the bodies.
2. Iron on the back side of the bright blue fabric, following the manufacturer's instructions.
3. Cut out the bodies on the traced lines.
4. Cut the remaining bright blue fabric into 2" strips for the inner border.

From the black and white striped fabric, cut the dragonfly wings:
1. Make templates for the upper and lower wings.
2. Fold the black and white striped fabric in half, right sides together. Press. Using the wing templates, trace the upper and lower wings on the folded fabric (48 sets of each).

3. Cut one traced wing from both layers of fabric to create a wing set. Pin the two layers together and set aside. **(Fig. 1)** Repeat for each set of wings.

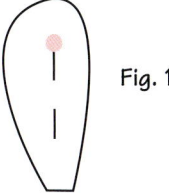

Two pieces of wing fabric, right sides together, makes one wing set

From the lime green fabric, cut:
- Six 2½" strips to be pieced for the second inner border

From the purple print fabric, cut:
- Six 3½" strips to be pieced for the outer border
- Seven 2¼" strips for binding.

MAKING THE BLOCKS

Follow **Piecing and Pressing**, page 69, to make the blocks. Refer to the **Sew-And-Flip Technique**, page 77, to make the Frog Blocks.

DRAGONFLY BLOCKS

Following the **Dragonfly Block Assembly Diagram**, iron four dragonfly bodies on one 14½" background square. Repeat, using the remaining 14½" background squares and dragonfly bodies to make six blocks in all. Buttonhole stitch around each dragonfly body with bright blue embroidery floss.

FROG BLOCKS

You will make six frog blocks in all--two from each of the three bright green colors. The instructions in this section make one frog. Repeat to make the other five.

Frog Feet:

Be aware from which corner the directions tell you to sew a given block.
1. Place one 1½" background square on one 1½" x 7½" frog #1 rectangle, right sides together. Sew along the diagonal from the upper right corner to the lower left corner. **(Fig. 2a)**
2. Open out the triangle formed and finger press the seam open. Check that the corners are aligned squarely. Flip the triangle back down and trim away the excess fabric, leaving a ¼" seam allowance. **(Fig. 2b)**
3. Flip up the background square and press. **(Fig. 2c)**
4. Repeat with another 1½" background square on the other end of the piece, sewing from the upper left corner to the lower right corner. **(Fig. 2d)**
5. Repeat with another 1½" x 7½" frog #1 rectangle and two 1½" background squares to make the other foot.

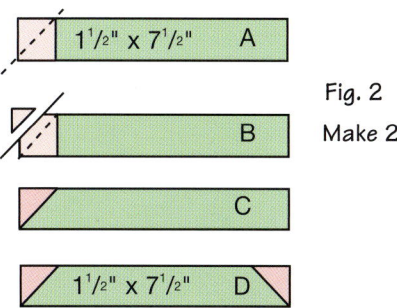

Fig. 2 Make 2

Frog Body:
1. Place one 1½" background square on the lower left corner of one 3½" x 14½" frog #1 rectangle, right sides together. Sew along the diagonal from the upper left corner to the lower right corner.
2. Open out the triangle formed and finger press the seam open. Check that the corners are aligned squarely. Flip the triangle back down and trim away the excess fabric, leaving a ¼" seam allowance.
3. Flip up the background square and press.
4. Repeat with another 1½" background square on the lower right corner, sewing from the upper right corner to the lower left corner. **(Fig. 3)**

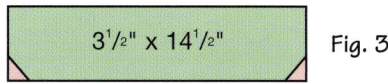

Fig. 3

5. Place one 1½" background square on the left side of one 1½" x 6½" frog #1 rectangle, right sides together. Sew along the diagonal from the upper right corner to the lower left corner.
6. Open out the triangle and finger press the seam open. Check that the corners are aligned squarely. Flip the triangle back down and trim away the excess fabric, leaving a ¼" seam allowance.
7. Flip up the background square and press. **(Fig. 4)**

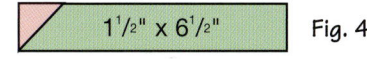

Fig. 4

8. Place one 1½" background square on the right side of one 1½" x 5½" frog #1 rectangle, right sides together. Sew along the diagonal from the upper left corner to the lower right corner.
9. Open out the triangle and finger press the seam open. Check that the corners are aligned squarely. Flip the triangle back down and trim away the excess fabric, leaving a ¼" seam allowance.
10. Flip up the background square and press. (Fig. 5)

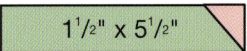
Fig. 5

11. Place one 1½" frog #1 square on one 1½" x 3½" hot pink rectangle, right sides together. Sew along the diagonal from the upper left corner to the lower right corner.
12. Open out the triangle and finger press the seam open. Check that the corners are aligned squarely. Flip the triangle back down and trim away the excess fabric, leaving a ¼" seam allowance.
13. Flip up the frog #1 square and press.
14. Repeat with another 1½" frog #1 square on the other side of the piece, sewing from the upper right corner to the lower left corner. (Fig. 6)

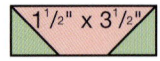
Fig. 6

15. Sew the pieces from Figs. 4, 5, and 6 together. (Fig. 7)

Fig. 7

Frog Head:
1. Place one 1½" background square on the left side of one 1½" x 4½" frog #1 rectangle, right sides together. Sew along the diagonal from the upper right corner to the lower left corner.
2. Open out the triangle and finger press the seam open. Check that the corners are aligned squarely. Flip the triangle back down and trim away the excess fabric, leaving a ¼" seam allowance.
3. Flip up the background square and press. (Fig. 8)

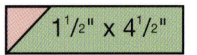
Fig. 8

4. Place one 1½" background square on the right side of one 1½" x 3½" frog #1 rectangle, right sides together. Sew along the diagonal from the upper left corner to the lower right corner.
5. Open out the triangle and finger press the seam open. Check that the corners are aligned squarely. Flip the triangle back down and trim away the excess fabric, leaving a ¼" seam allowance.
6. Flip up the background square and press. (Fig. 9)

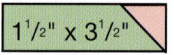
Fig. 9

7. Sew the pieces from Figs. 8 and 9 together with a 1½" x 3½" hot pink rectangle between them. (Fig. 10)

Fig. 10

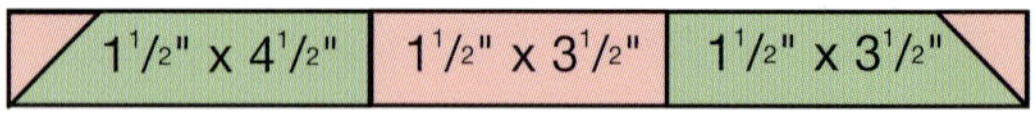

8. Place one 1½" background square on the lower left corner of one 2½" x 10½" frog #1 rectangle, right sides together. Sew along the diagonal from the upper left corner to the lower right corner.
9. Open out the triangle formed and finger press the seam open. Check that the corners are aligned squarely. Flip the triangle back down and trim away the excess fabric, leaving a ¼" seam allowance.
10. Flip up the background square and press. Repeat with another 1½" background square on the lower right corner, sewing from the upper right corner to the lower left corner. (Fig. 11)

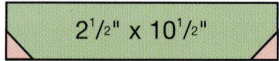
Fig. 11

Lower Left Eye Section (Fig. 12a.):
1. Place one 1½" background square on the top left corner of one 2½" frog #1 square, right sides together. Sew along the diagonal from the upper right corner to the lower left corner.
2. Open out the triangle formed and finger press the seam open. Check that the corners are aligned squarely. Flip the triangle back down and trim away the excess fabric, leaving a ¼" seam allowance.

3. Flip up the background square and press. Repeat with one 1½" white square on the top right side, sewing from the upper left corner to the lower right corner

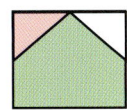 Fig. 12A

Lower Right Eye Section (Fig. 12b):
1. Place one 1½" white square on the top left corner of one 2½" frog #1 square, right sides together. Sew along the diagonal from the upper right corner to the lower left corner.
2. Open out the triangle formed and finger press the seam open. Check that the corners are aligned squarely. Flip the triangle back down and trim away the excess fabric, leaving a ¼" seam allowance.
3. Flip up the white square and press. Repeat with one 1½" background square on the top right side, but this time, sew from the upper left corner to the lower right corner.

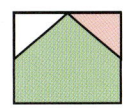 Fig. 12B

Eyeballs:
1. Sew one 1½" black square to the top of one 1½" frog #1 square. Repeat to make two sets. **(Fig. 13)**

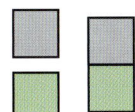 Fig. 13 Make 2

2. Place one 1½" white square on one 1½" x 2½" frog #1 rectangle, right sides together. Sew along the diagonal from the upper right corner to the lower left corner.
3. Open out the triangle formed and finger press the seam open. Check that the corners are aligned squarely. Flip the triangle back down and trim away the excess fabric, leaving a ¼" seam allowance.
4. Flip up the white square up and press. Repeat with one 1½" black square on the other side of the piece, sewing from the upper right corner to the lower left corner. **(Fig. 14a)**

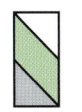 Fig. 14A

5. Place one 1½" black square on one 1½" x 2½" frog #1 rectangle, right sides together. Sew along the diagonal from the upper left corner to the lower right corner.
6. Open out the triangle formed and finger press the seam open. Check that the corners are aligned squarely. Flip the triangle back down and trim away the excess fabric, leaving a ¼" seam allowance.
7. Flip up the black square and press. Repeat with one 1½" white square on the other side of the piece, sewing from the upper left corner to the lower right corner. **(Fig. 14b)**

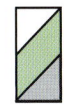 Fig. 14B

Lower Eye Section Assembly:
Sew the pieces from Figs. 12, 13, and 14 together with one 2½" frog #1 square in the center. See **Fig. 15**.

Fig. 15
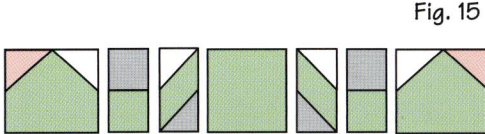

Upper Eye Section (Fig. 16):
1. Place one 1½" frog #1 square on one 1½" x 3½" white rectangle, right sides together. Sew along the diagonal from the upper right corner to the lower left corner.
2. Open out the triangle formed and finger press the seam open. Check that the corners are aligned squarely. Flip the triangle back down and trim away the excess fabric, leaving a ¼" seam allowance.
3. Flip up the frog #1 square and press. Repeat with another 1½" frog #1 square on the other end of the piece, sewing from the upper left corner to the lower right corner.

4. Repeat to make two upper eyes.

Fig. 16
Make 2

Upper Eyelid Section (Fig. 17):
1. Place one 1½" background square on one 1½" x 3½" frog #1 rectangle, right sides together. Sew along the diagonal from the upper right corner to the lower left corner.
2. Open out the triangle formed and finger press the seam open. Check that the corners are aligned squarely. Flip the triangle back down and trim away the excess fabric, leaving a ¼" seam allowance.
3. Flip up the background square and press. Repeat with one 1½" background square on the other end of the piece, sewing from the upper left corner to the lower right corner.
4. Repeat to make two Upper Eye Lids

Fig. 17
Make 2

Upper Eye Section Assembly:
1. Sew the upper eyelid section above the upper eye section. **(Fig. 18)**

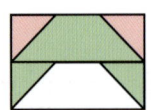
Fig. 18
Make 2

2. Sew the upper eye and eyelid piece from the previous step together with two 1½" x 2½" background rectangles and one 2½" background square, using **Fig. 19** as a guide.

Fig. 19

Dragonfly Wings:
Sew around each dragonfly wing set, leaving a 2" opening on one side for turning. Turn all the wings right side out. Use a small dowel or turning tool to shape the edges. Topstitch the opening closed. There should be 48 upper wings and 48 lower wings.

ASSEMBLING THE QUILT TOP:
BLOCKS:
1. Follow **Frog Block Assembly Diagram** to make six frog blocks in all (two from each bright green fabric).
2. Sew the blocks together, alternating them with the dragonfly blocks. Use the project photo as a guide.

BORDERS:
1. Measure the quilt top and piece the bright blue inner borders from the 2" strips. Sew them to the sides, top, and bottom of the quilt top.
2. Measure the quilt top and piece the lime green second inner borders from the 2½" strips. Sew them to the sides, top, and bottom.
3. Measure the quilt top and piece the purple print outer borders from the 3½" strips. Sew them to the sides, top, and bottom.

COMPLETING THE QUILT:
1. Follow **Quilting**, page 71, to mark, layer, and quilt as desired.
2. When the top is completely quilted, position the dragonfly wings on each dragonfly body (two upper wings and two lower wings on each). Pin in place with safety pins.
3. Quilt through the center of each wing **(Fig. 20)**, pg 33. Remove the safety pins.
4. Follow Making **Straight Grain Binding**, page 73, and **Attaching Binding with Mitered Corners**, page 73, to attach binding to quilt.

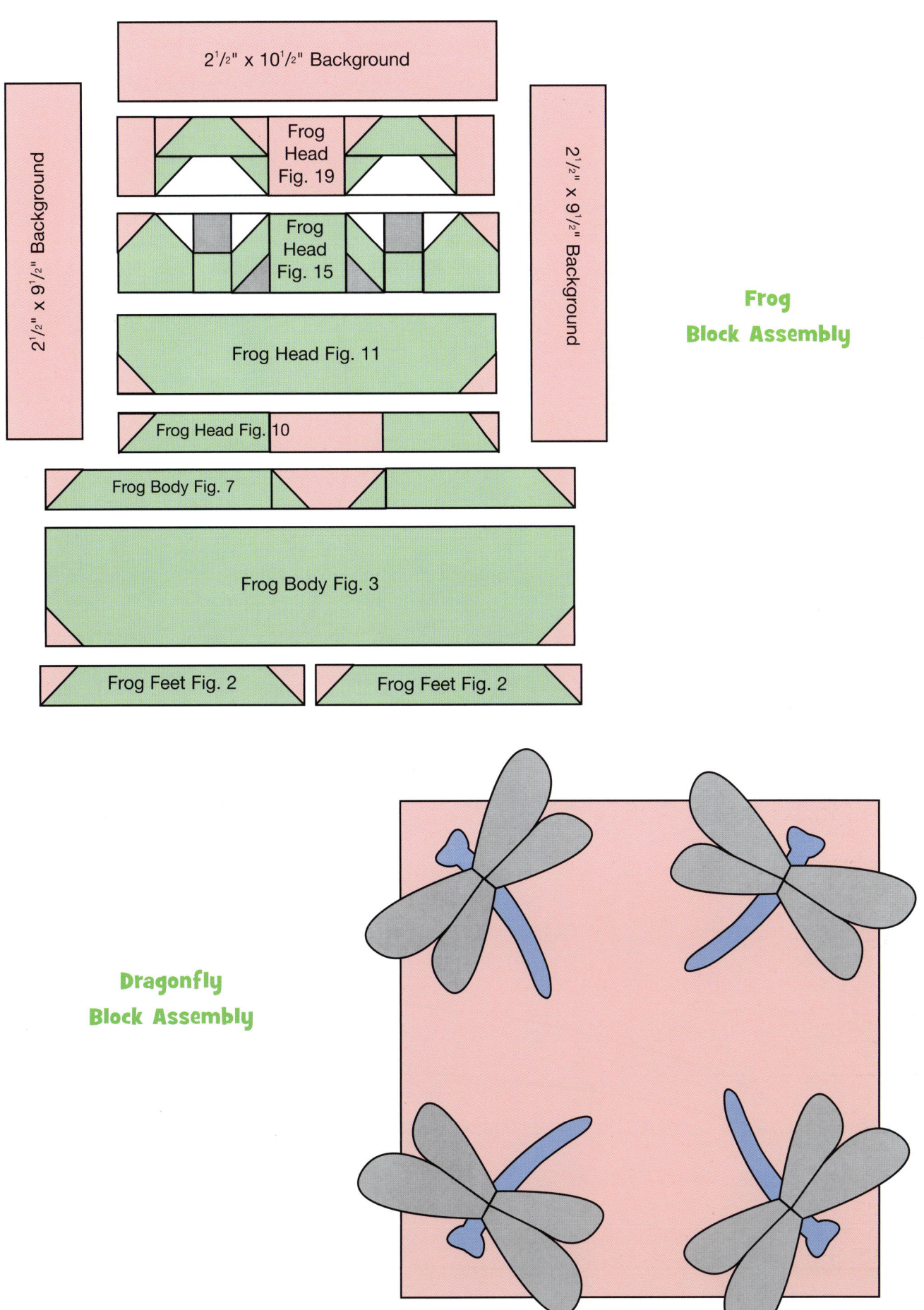

Dragonfly templates

Dragonfly body pattern is reversed for fusible appliqué

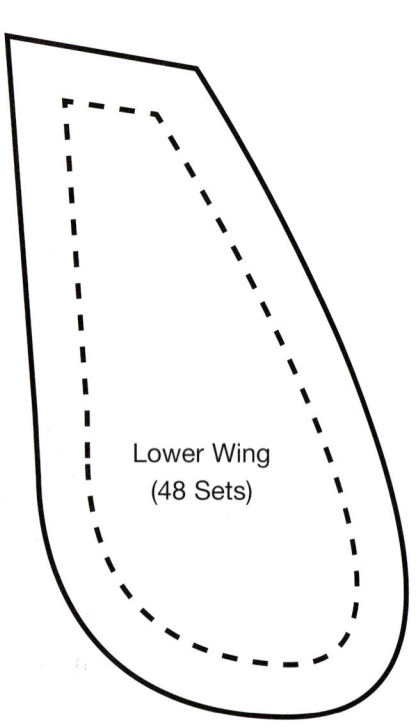

Lower Wing
(48 Sets)

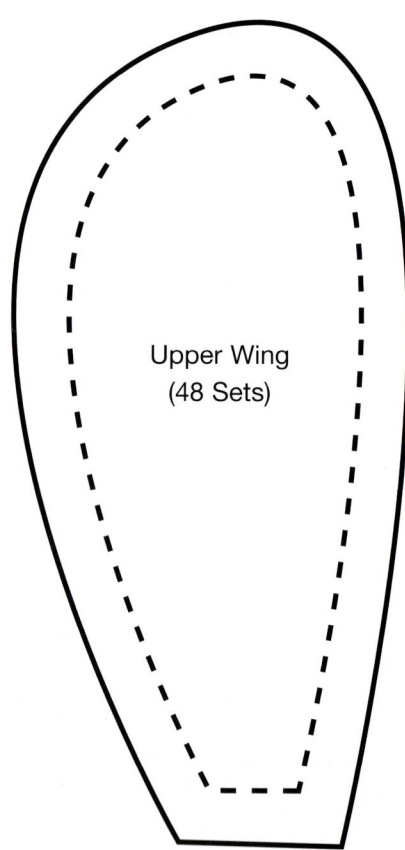

Upper Wing
(48 Sets)

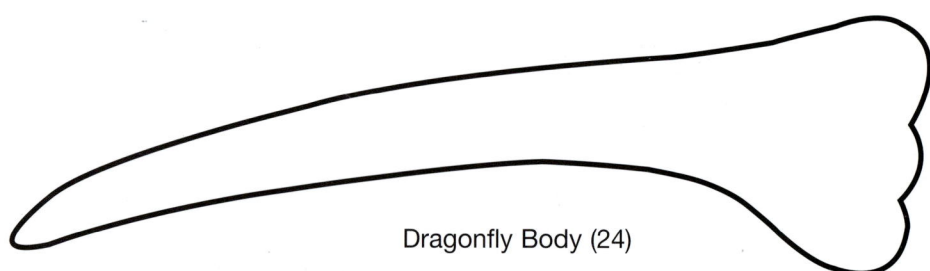

Dragonfly Body (24)

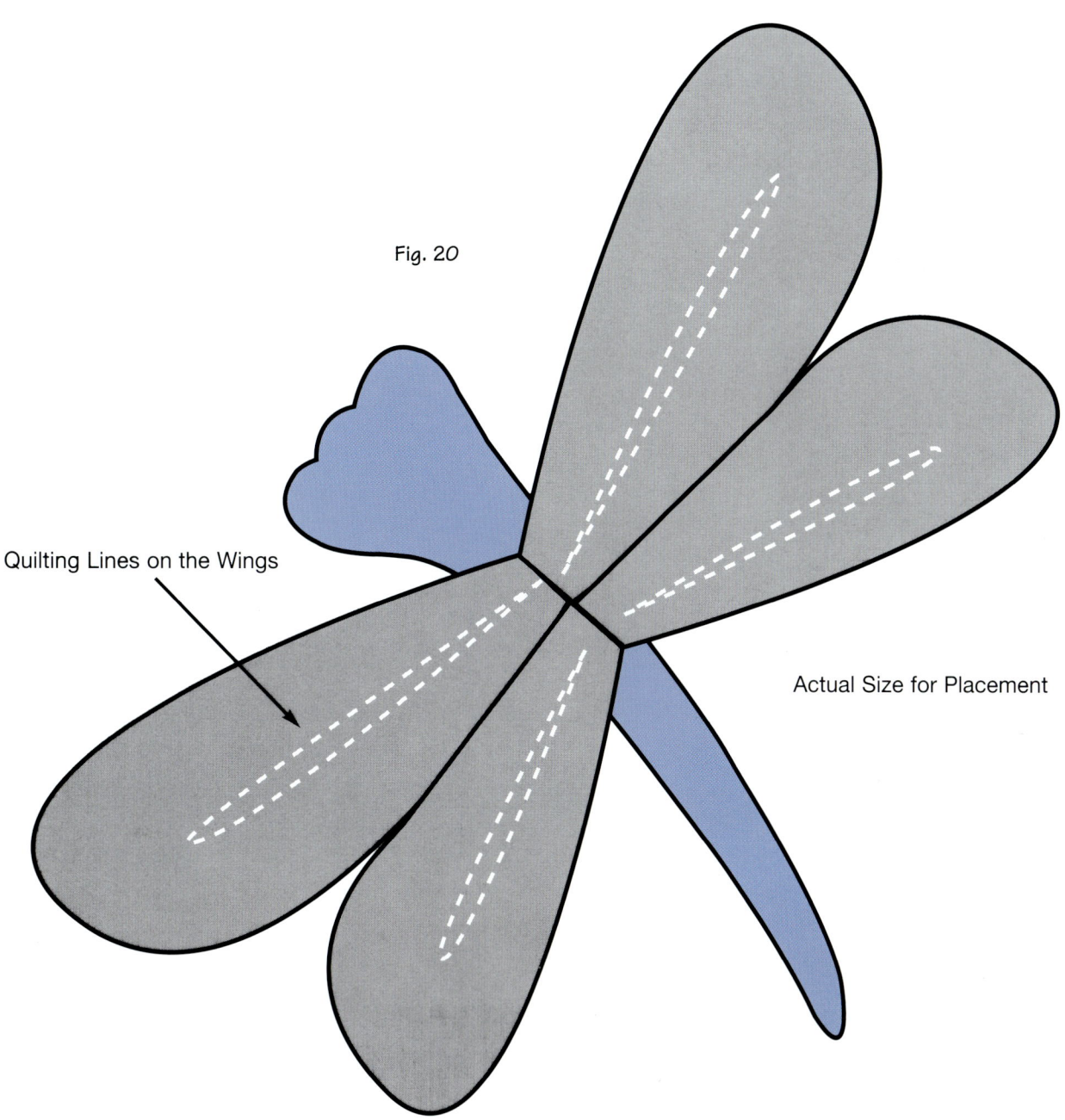

Fig. 20

Quilting Lines on the Wings

Actual Size for Placement

Quilt Top Diagram

34

Fishy Recess

Supplies Needed:

FABRIC:

2 yards (1.82 m)	Background - Blue Print
1/4 yard (23 cm)	Center Squares (6 Blocks) - Yellow Print
5/8 yard (57 cm)	Fish - Purple
5/8 yard (57 cm)	Fish - Pink
1/2 yard (46 cm)	Sashing - Lime Green
1 yard (.91 m)	Sashing & Binding - Dk. Green
1 yard (.91 m)	Inner Border & Fish Tails - Yellow
2 yards (1.82 m)	Outer Border - Fish Print
1/4 yd. (23 cm)	Eyes - White
4 1/2 yards (4.1 m)	Backing - Coordinating Print

Other Supplies:

24 Black Buttons, 3/8" (small fish eyes)
6 Black Buttons, 5/8" (large fish eyes)
65" x 79" (165 cm x 201 cm) Rectangle of Batting
1 Skein each of Embroidery Floss in Black, Purple and Yellow
1/4 yd. (23 cm) Paper-backed Fusible Web
Stabilizer

Fishy Recess

By Heidi Pridemore

Finished Size: 58" x 72"

Pattern Level: Advanced Beginner

All seam allowances are 1/4".

Please read all directions before beginning and press carefully step-by-step.

CUTTING OUT THE PIECES

All measurements include a 1/4" seam allowance. Follow **Rotary Cutting**, page 68, to cut fabric.

From blue print background fabric, cut:
- Three 2 7/8" strips. Cut the strips to make thirty-six 2 7/8" squares. Cut twenty four of the squares diagonally to make triangles.
- One 12 1/2" strip. Cut into six 2 1/2" x 12 1/2" pieces and six 1 1/2" x 12 1/2" pieces.
- Four 6 1/2" strips. Cut into twelve 4 1/2" x 6 1/2" pieces, twelve 3 1/2" x 6 1/2" pieces and twelve 2 1/2" x 6 1/2" pieces.
- Three 4 1/2" strips. Cut into twenty-four 4 1/2" squares.

From yellow print fabric, cut:
- One 4 1/2" strip. Cut into six 4 1/2" squares.

From purple fabric, cut:
- One 2 7/8" strip. Cut into six 2 7/8" squares.
- Two 4 1/2" strips. Cut into twelve 4 1/2" squares.
- One 4 7/8" strip. Cut into six 4 7/8" squares. Cut each square diagonally to make twelve triangles.

From pink fabric, cut:
- One 2 7/8" strip. Cut into six 2 7/8" squares.
- Two 3 1/2" strips. Cut into twelve 3 1/2" squares.
- One 4 7/8" strip. Cut into six 4 7/8" squares. Cut each square diagonally to make twelve triangles.

From lime green fabric, cut:
- Four 2 1/2" strips. Cut into fifty-four 2 1/2" squares.

From dark green fabric, cut:
- Four 2 1/2" strips. Cut into fifty-four 2 1/2" squares.
- Seven 2 1/4" strips for binding.

From yellow fabric, cut:
- One 2 1/2" strip. Cut into twelve 2 1/2" squares.
- Six 3 1/2" strips for inner border.

From the fish print outer border fabric, cut:
- Three strips, 6" x width of fabric strips (for the top and bottom borders).
- Three strips, 6" x remaining length of fabric (for the side borders).

Note: These instructions are for cutting a directional fabric.

CUTTING OUT THE APPLIQUÉS

1. Trace the patterns for the fish eyes on the paper side of fusible web with a permanent marker or pencil, following the manufacturer's instructions. Make six from A and 24 from B, page 41.
2. Roughly cut out each shape from the fusible web.
3. Iron the shapes on the back side of the white fabric.
4. Cut out each shape on the traced lines. Remove backing

MAKING THE BLOCKS

Follow **Piecing and Pressing**, page 69, to make the blocks. Parts of the fish blocks are made using a "flip-and-sew" technique. Before you begin sewing, see the **Sew-and-Flip Technique**, page 77.

BLOCKS WITH SMALL FISH:

1. Place one 2⅞" purple square on one 2⅞" background square, right sides together. Draw a diagonal line through the center of the top block. **(Fig. 1)**

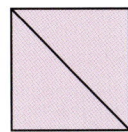
Fig. 1

2. Sew ¼" away from each side of the drawn diagonal line. **(Fig. 2)**

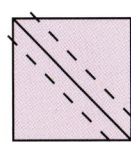
Fig. 2

3. Cut the squares across the drawn diagonal line to make two half-square triangles. **(Fig. 3)**

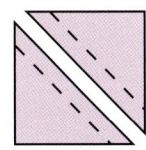
Fig. 3

4. Open each half-square triangle to make a square. (Each is a purple tail unit.) Press.
5. Repeat steps 1 though 4, using five more 2⅞" purple squares and five more 2⅞" background squares to make twelve purple tail units in all.
6. Repeat steps 1 though 4, using six 2⅞" background squares and six 2⅞" pink squares to make twelve pink tail units.
7. Piece together two 2⅞" background triangles, one 4⅞" purple fish triangle, and one purple tail unit to make one small fish. **(Fig. 4)** Using Fig. 4 as a guide, make twelve purple fish and twelve pink fish.

Fig. 4

8. Following the Small Fish Block Layout Diagram **(Fig. 5)**, take two **pink** fish, two **purple** fish, one 4½" **yellow** center square, and four 4½" background squares to make one Small Fish Block. Make six Small Fish Blocks in all.

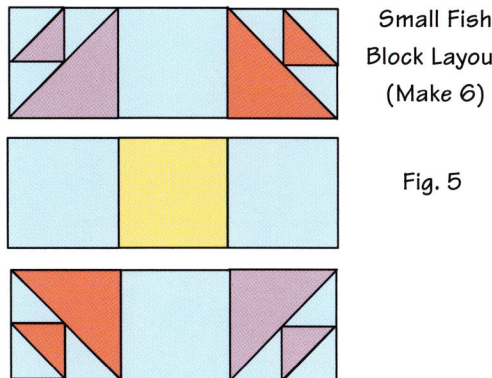
Small Fish Block Layout (Make 6)
Fig. 5

9. Fuse an eye (Pattern B) to each fish and blanket stitch around each eye using black thread. Refer to the photo, page 43, for placement.

BLOCKS WITH LARGE FISH:

1. Place one 4½" purple square on the right end of one 4½" x 6½" background piece, right sides together. Using the sew-and-flip technique, sew along the diagonal to make one Unit 1-A. **(Fig. 6)**

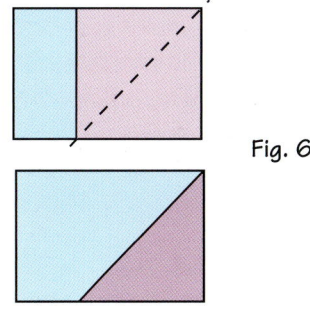
Fig. 6

2. Place one 4½" purple square on the left end of one 4½" x 6½" background piece, right sides together. Using the sew-and-flip technique, sew along the diagonal to make one Unit 1-B. **(Fig. 7)**

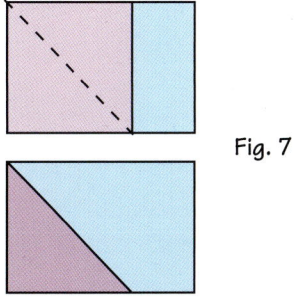
Fig. 7

3. Place one 3½" pink square on the right end of one 3½" x 6½" background piece, right sides together. Using the sew-and-flip technique, sew along the diagonal to make one Unit 2-A. **(Fig. 8)**

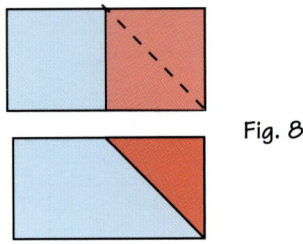

Fig. 8

4. Place one 3½" pink square on the left end of one 3½" x 6½" background piece, right sides together. Using the sew-and-flip technique, sew along the diagonal to make one Unit 2-B. **(Fig. 9)**

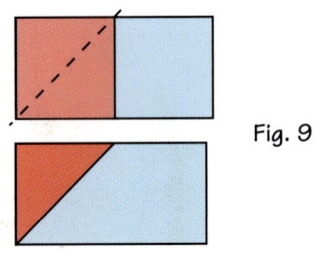

Fig. 9

5. Place one 2½" yellow square on the right end of one 2½" x 6½" background piece, right sides together. Using the sew-and-flip technique, sew along the diagonal to make one Unit 3-A. **(Fig. 10)**

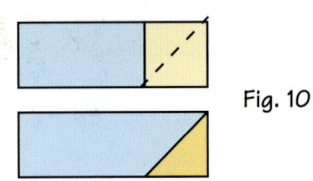

Fig. 10

6. Place one 2½" yellow square on the left end of one 2½" x 6½" background piece, right sides together. Using the sew-and-flip technique, sew along the diagonal to make one Unit 3-B. **(Fig. 11)**

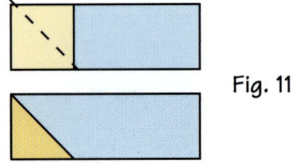

Fig. 11

7. Following the Large Fish Block Assembly Diagram **(Fig. 12)**, take one each of Units 1A, 1B, 2A, 2B, 3A, and 3B; one 2½" x 12½" background piece; and one 1½" x 12½" background piece. Make one Large Fish Block.

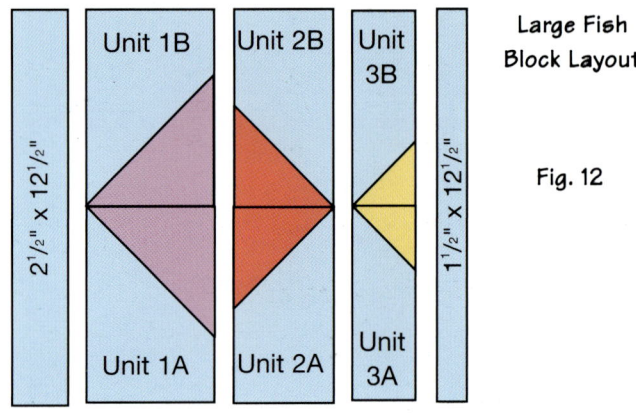

Large Fish Block Layout

Fig. 12

8. Repeat Step 1 through 7 to make six Large Fish Blocks in all.
9. Fuse an eye (Pattern A) to each fish and blanket stitch around each eye using black thread. Refer to the photo, page 43, for placement.

MAKING THE SASHING

1. To make the sashing that separates the blocks vertically, sew together three 2½" lime green squares and three 2½" dark green squares, alternating colors. **(Fig. 13)** Repeat to make eight in all.

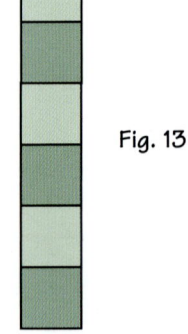

Fig. 13

2. To make the sashing that goes between the rows of blocks horizontally, sew together ten 2½" lime green squares and ten 2½" dark green squares, alternating colors. Make three in all.

ASSEMBLING THE QUILT TOP

Use the **Quilt Top Diagram** and the project photo as guides.

1. Piece 3½" yellow fabric strips together to make the inner border. Cut two 3½" x 54½" side inner borders and two 3½" x 46½" top/bottom inner borders.
2. From the outer border fabric, piece two strips, each 6" x 57½" for the top and bottom borders.
3. From the outer border fabric, piece two 6" x 60½" for the side borders.
4. Using the **Quilt Top Diagram** as a guide, assemble the blocks.
5. Sew one side inner border to each side of the assembled blocks, then add top and bottom borders.
6. Sew one 6" x 60½" outer border to each side.
7. Sew one 6" x 57½" outer border to the top and bottom.
8. Backstitch mouths and "stripes" on each fish, using 2 strands of embroidery floss and referring to photo, page 43, for placement.

COMPLETING THE QUILT

1. Follow **Quilting**, page 71, to mark, layer, and quilt as desired.
2. Follow **Making Straight Grain Binding**, page 73, and **Attaching Binding with Mitered Corners**, page 73, to piece and attach the dark green binding to the quilt.
3. Sew a ⅜" button to the eye of each small fish.
4. Sew a ⅝" button to the eye of each large fish.

Fish Eye Patterns

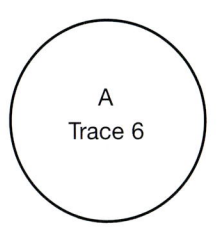

A
Trace 6

B
Trace 24

Quilt Top Diagram

43

Sundae Delight

Supplies Needed:

FABRIC:

1 ½ yds. (1.4 m)	Background - Light Blue
¼ yd. (23 cm)	Ice Cream - Yellow
¼ yd. (23 cm)	Hot Fudge & Stems - Brown
⅛ yd. (11 cm)	Cherries - Red
¼ yd. (23 cm)	Ice Cream - Peach
¼ yd. (23 cm)	Ice Cream - Grape
¼ yd. (23 cm)	Ice Cream - Green
¼ yd. (23 cm)	Ice Cream - Pink
¼ yd. (23 cm)	Ice Cream - Blue
¼ yd. (23 cm)	Ice Cream Cone - Tan
¼ yd. (23 cm)	Ice Cream Dishes - Lavender
¼ yd. (23 cm)	Whipped Cream Topping - White
1 yd. (.91 m)	Sashing & Binding - Small Print
1 ½ yds. (1.4 m)	Backing - Coordinating Print

Other Supplies:

2 yds. (1.82 m) Paper-backed Fusible Web
Stabilizer
40" x 54" (102 cm x 137 cm) Rectangle of Batting
Bugle Beads - Various Colors
Appliqué Pressing Sheet

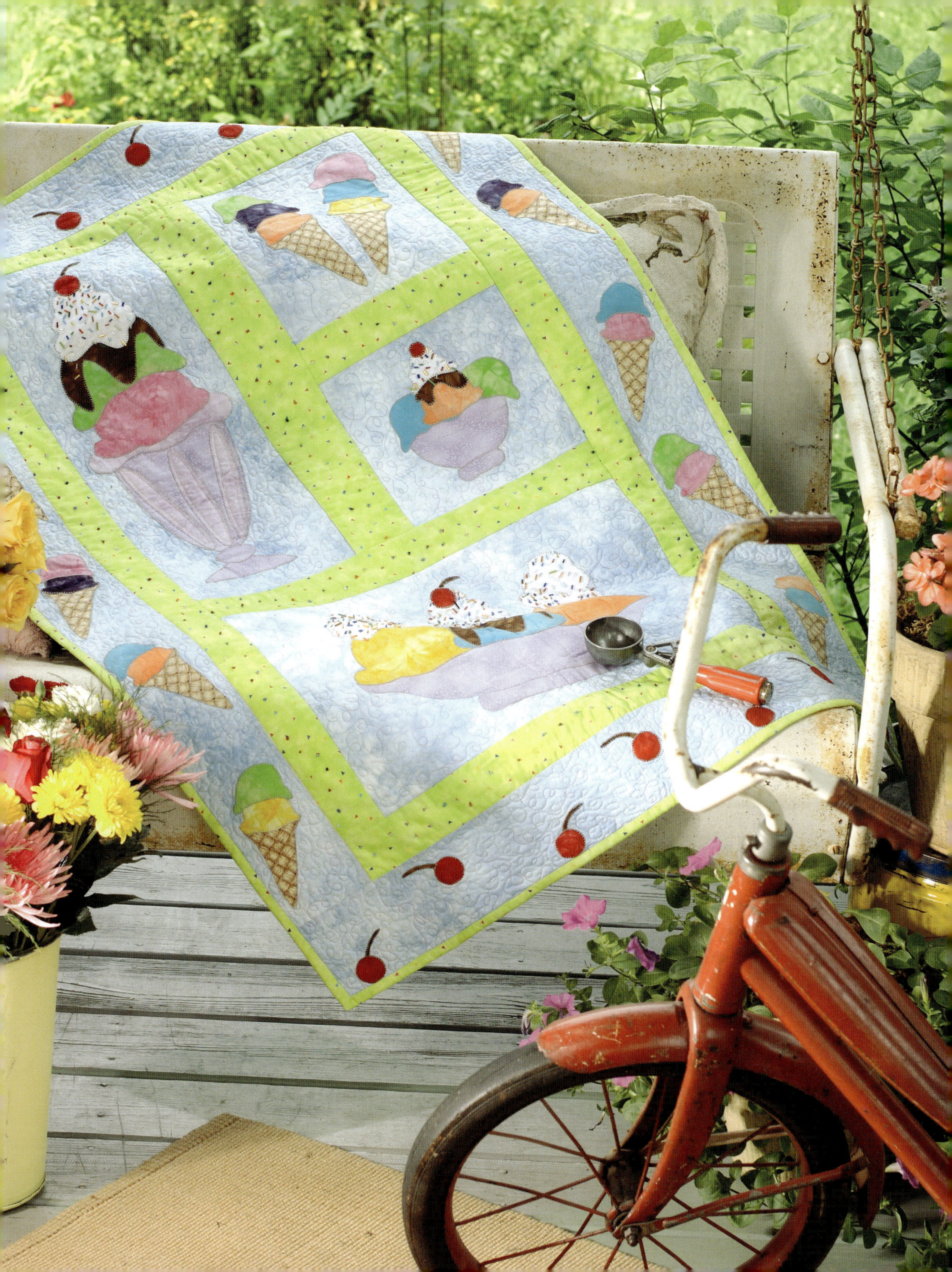

Sundae Delight

By Heidi Pridemore

Finished Size: 37" x 51"
Pattern Level: Advanced Beginner
All seam allowances are 1/4".
Please read all directions before beginning and press carefully step-by-step.

Note: This Pattern has been written to use the fusible web appliqué technique. I recommend using an appliqué pressing sheet for easier assembly.

CUTTING OUT THE PIECES

All measurements include a 1/4" seam allowance. Follow **Rotary Cutting**, page 68, to cut fabric. Refer to **Preparing Fusible Appliqués**, page 70, to use patterns, pages 47-53.

From the light blue background fabric, cut:
- One piece 8 1/2" x 20 1/2" (background 1)
- One piece 20 1/2" x 12 1/2" (background 2)
- One piece 9 1/2" x 8 1/2" (background 3)
- One piece 9 1/2" x 10 1/2" (background 4)
- Two pieces 6 1/2" x 38 1/2" (side borders)
- Two pieces 6 1/2" x 36 1/2" (top border, bottom border)

From the small print, cut:
- Two pieces 2 1/2" x 34 1/2" (sashing A and C)
- One piece 3 1/2" x 20 1/2" (sashing B)
- One piece 2 1/2" x 20 1/2" (sashing D)
- Two pieces 2 1/2" x 24 1/2" (sashing E and F)
- One piece 2 1/2" x 9 1/2" (sashing G)
- Five 2 1/4" strips (binding)

From the remaining fabrics:
1. Trace the patterns and labels on the paper side of the fusible web, following the manufacturer's instructions. Roughly cut out each shape from the fusible web and iron it on the back side of the fabric listed on each pattern. For the cherries on the top and bottom borders, trace 14 cherries and stems from Sundae #1 patterns. For the cones on the side borders, trace 10 cones using the small scoop and small cone patterns, pages 52-53.
2. Cut out each shape on the outline.

ASSEMBLING THE QUILT TOP

BLOCKS & SASHING:

1. Following the placement diagrams and using an appliqué pressing sheet, assemble sundae #1. Press and remove from sheet. Repeat to assemble all sundaes, cherries, and ice cream cones.
2. Following the **Quilt Top Diagram**, iron each sundae and ice cream cone on the appropriate background or border strip.
3. Finish all raw edges with a decorative stitch, such as the buttonhole or satin stitch.
4. Following the **Quilt Top Diagram**, sew background 4 to the top of sashing G.
5. Sew background 3 to the bottom of sashing G.
6. Sew sashing B to the left side of backgrounds 3 and 4.
7. Sew background 1 to the left side of sashing B. This completes the top unit.
8. Sew sashing D to the bottom of the top unit.
9. Sew background 2 to the bottom of sashing D.
10. Sew one 2 1/2" x 34 1/2" sashing piece A & C to each side.
11. Sew one 2 1/2" x 24 1/2" sashing piece E & F to the top and bottom.

BORDERS:
1. Sew the 6½" x 38½" ice cream cone border to each side.
2. Sew one 6½" x 36½" cherry border to the top and bottom.

COMPLETING THE QUILT
1. Follow **Quilting**, page 71, to mark, layer, and quilt as desired.
2. Follow **Making Straight Grain Binding**, page 73, and **Attaching Binding with Mitered Corners**, page 73, to attach binding to quilt.
3. Follow the **Beading Techniques** instructions on page 76 to decorate the sundaes and ice cream cones with bead "sprinkles."

Sundae #1 Assembly Drawing

Stem
Cherry
Whipped Cream
Hot Fudge
Large Scoop 1 Green
Large Scoop 2 Pink

Sundae Dish 1A
Sundae Dish 1B
Sundae Dish 1E
Sundae Dish 1F
Sundae Dish 1E
Sundae Dish 1C
Sundae Dish 1D

Sundae #2 Assembly Drawing

Whipped Cream
Large Scoop 2 - Yellow
Cherry w/stem
Whipped Cream
Hot Fudge
Large Scoop 2 - Blue
Whipped Cream
Large Scoop 2 - Peach
Sundae Dish 2A
Sundae Dish 2B

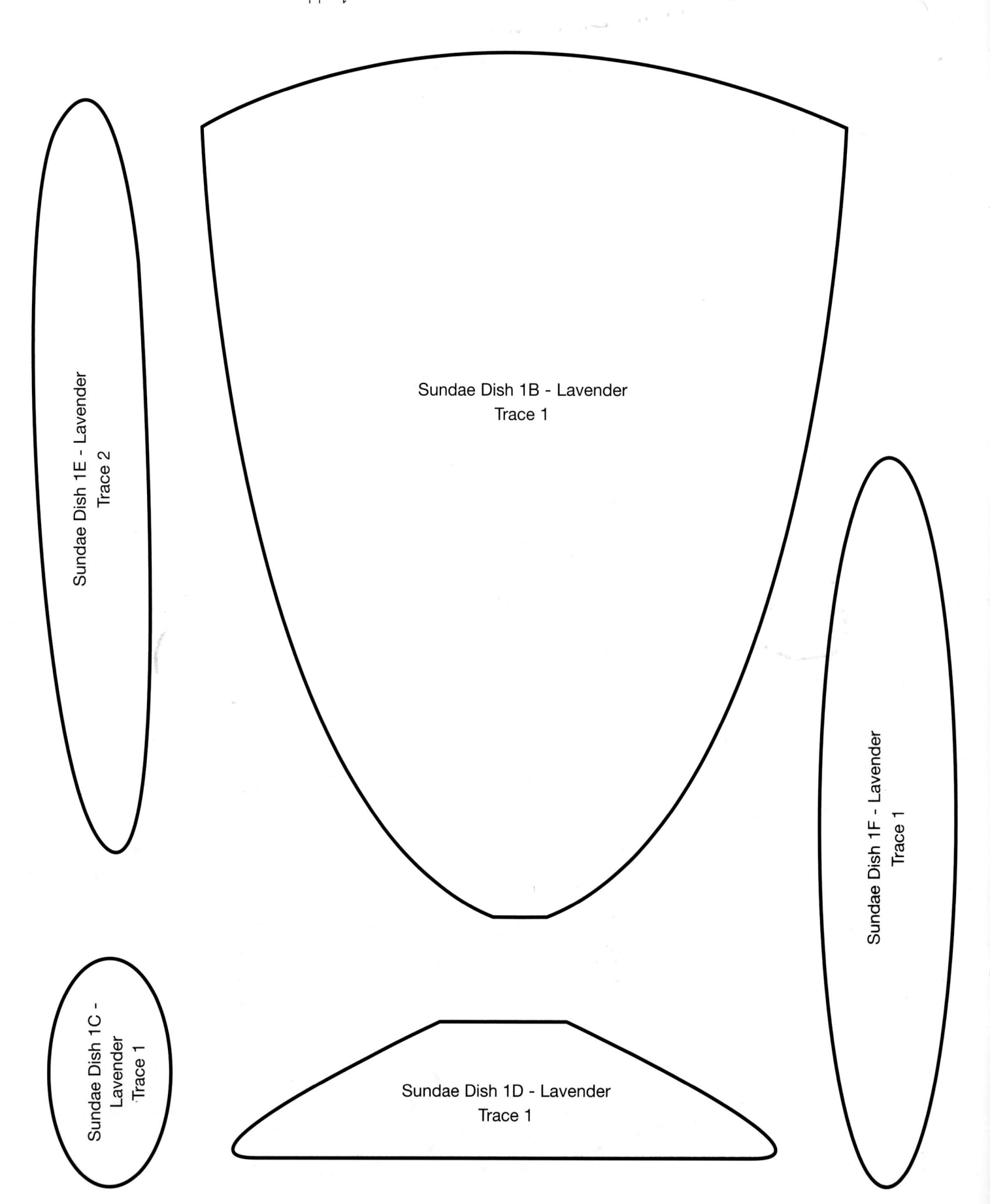

Sundae #1 & #2 Patterns
Patterns are reversed for fusible appliqué

Sundae Dish 1B - Lavender
Trace 1

Sundae Dish 1E - Lavender
Trace 2

Sundae Dish 1F - Lavender
Trace 1

Sundae Dish 1C - Lavender
Trace 1

Sundae Dish 1D - Lavender
Trace 1

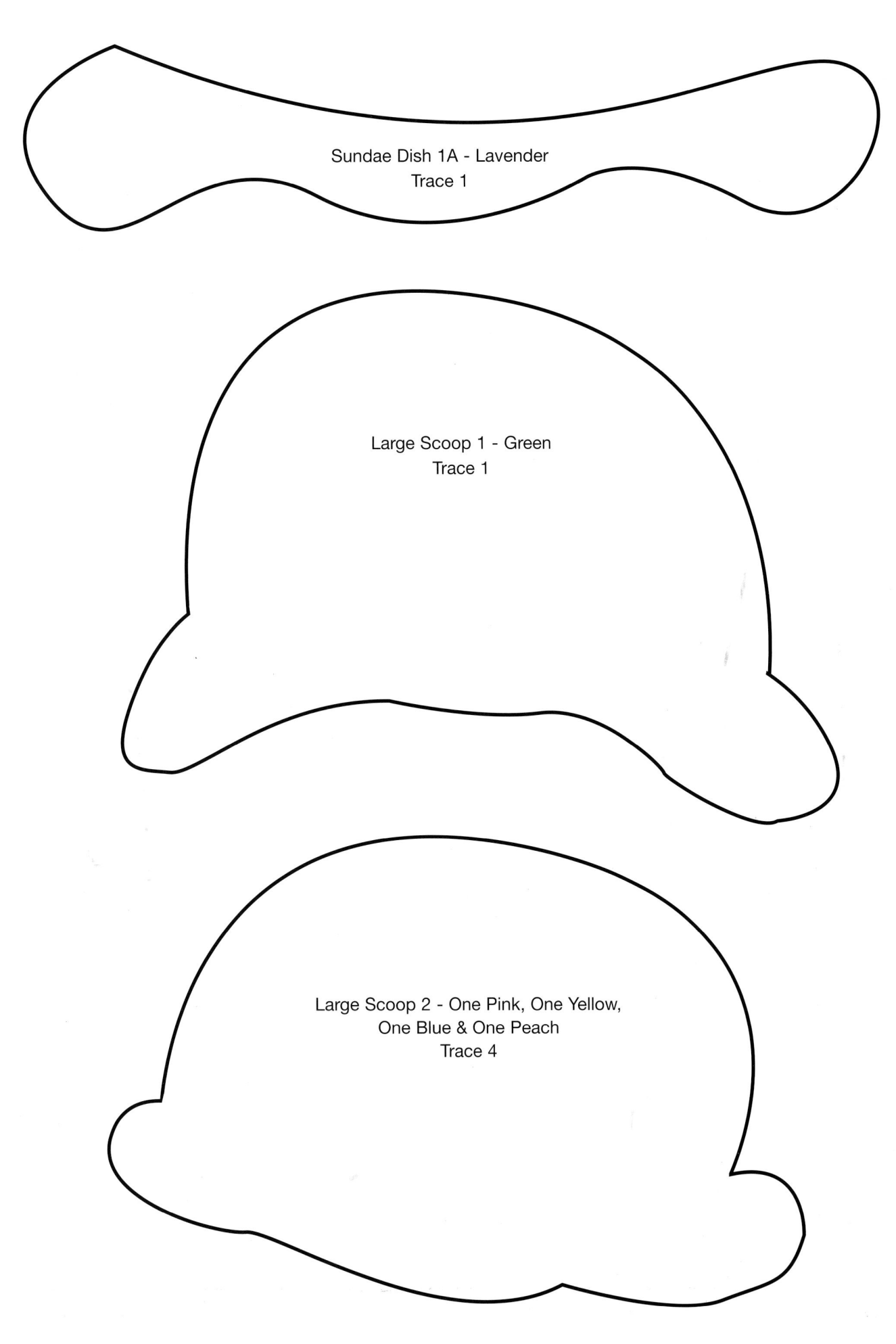

Sundae Dish 1A - Lavender
Trace 1

Large Scoop 1 - Green
Trace 1

Large Scoop 2 - One Pink, One Yellow,
One Blue & One Peach
Trace 4

Sundae #1 & #2 Patterns cont.

Patterns are reversed for fusible appliqué

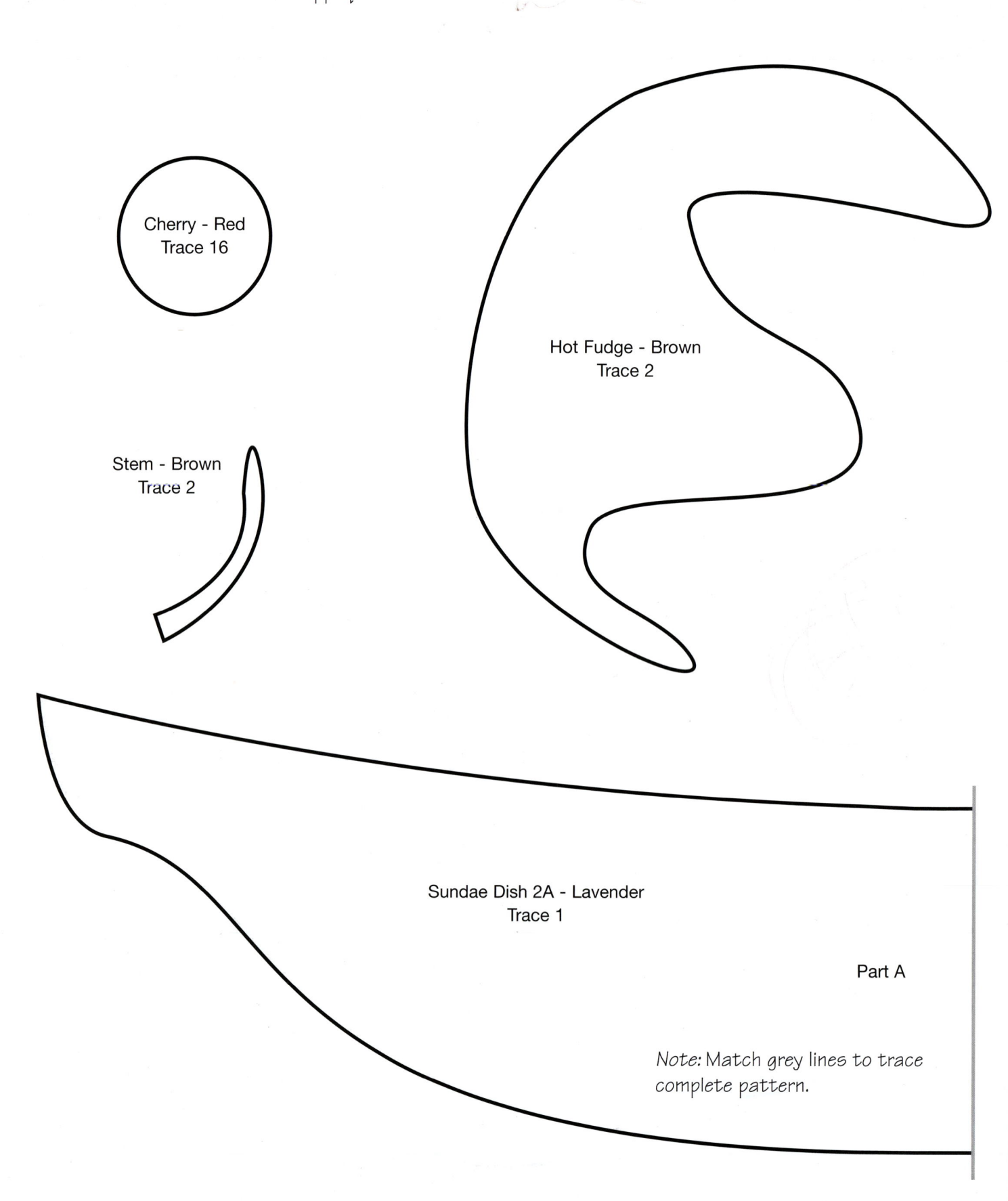

Cherry - Red
Trace 16

Hot Fudge - Brown
Trace 2

Stem - Brown
Trace 2

Sundae Dish 2A - Lavender
Trace 1

Part A

Note: Match grey lines to trace complete pattern.

50

Sundae Dish 2B - Lavender
Trace 1

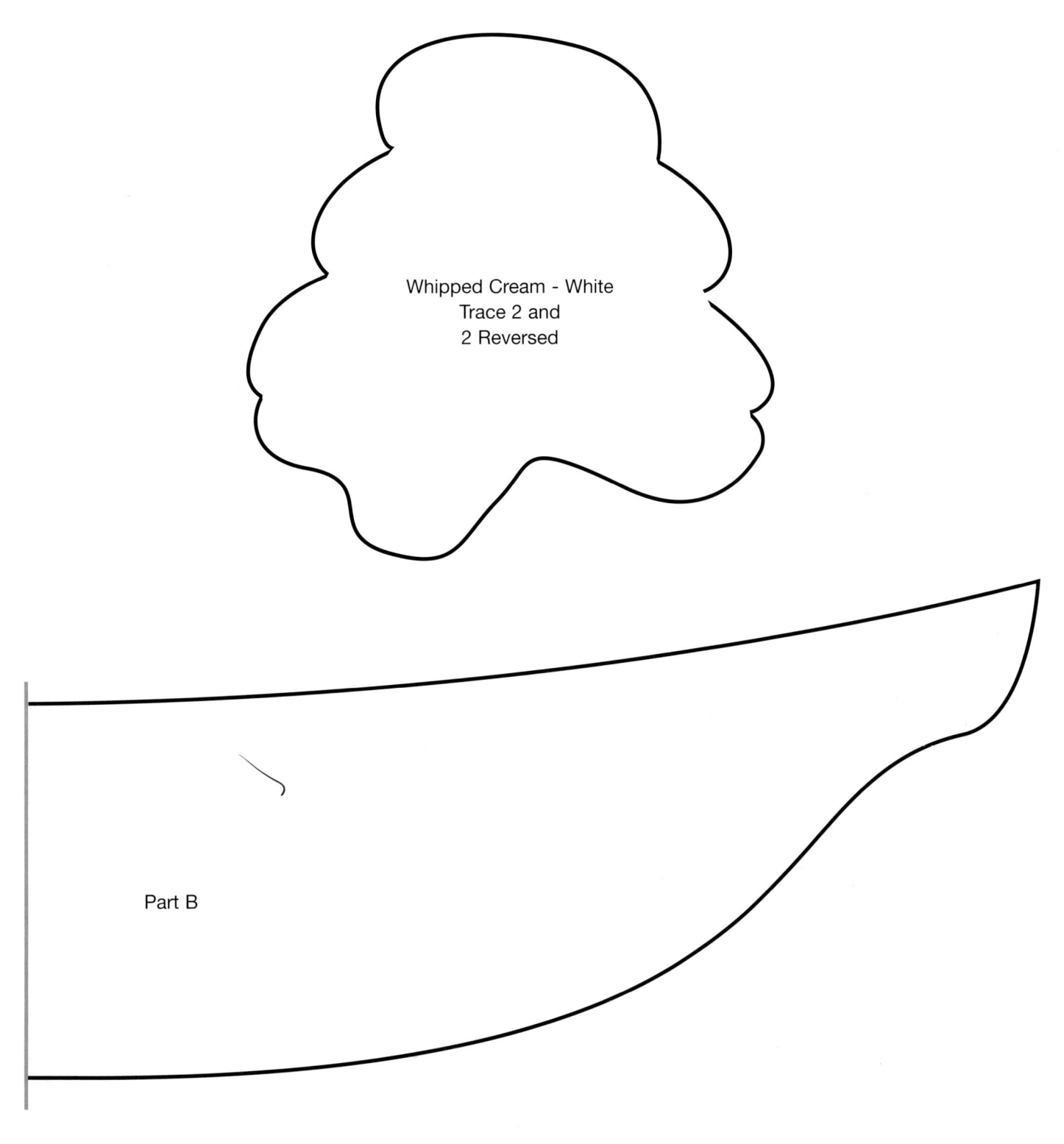

Whipped Cream - White
Trace 2 and
2 Reversed

Part B

51

Sundae #3 & Cones Assembly Drawings

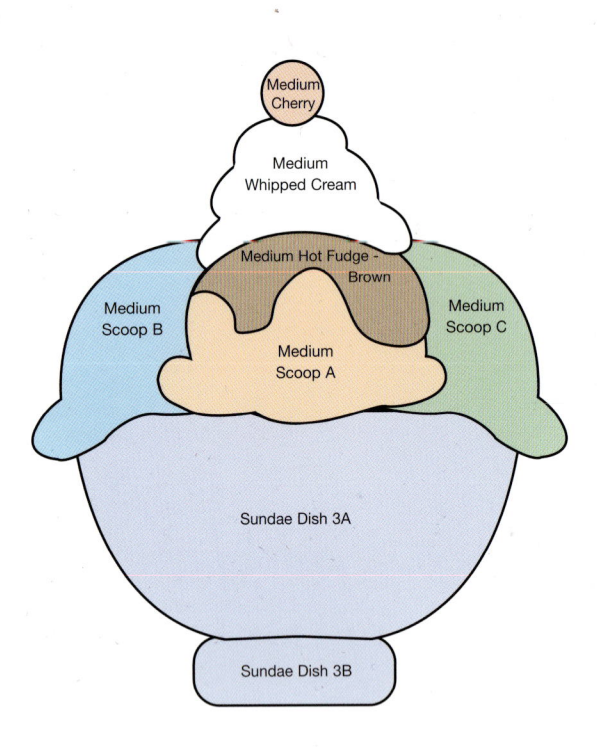

- Medium Cherry
- Medium Whipped Cream
- Medium Hot Fudge - Brown
- Medium Scoop B
- Medium Scoop C
- Medium Scoop A
- Sundae Dish 3A
- Sundae Dish 3B

- Small Scoop B Assorted Colors
- Small Scoop A Assorted Colors
- Small Cone Make 10

- Medium Scoop C One Pink & One Green
- Medium Scoop B One Purple & One Blue
- Medium Scoop A One Yellow & One Peach
- Medium Cone Make 2

Sundae #3 & Cones Patterns

Patterns are reversed for fusible appliqué

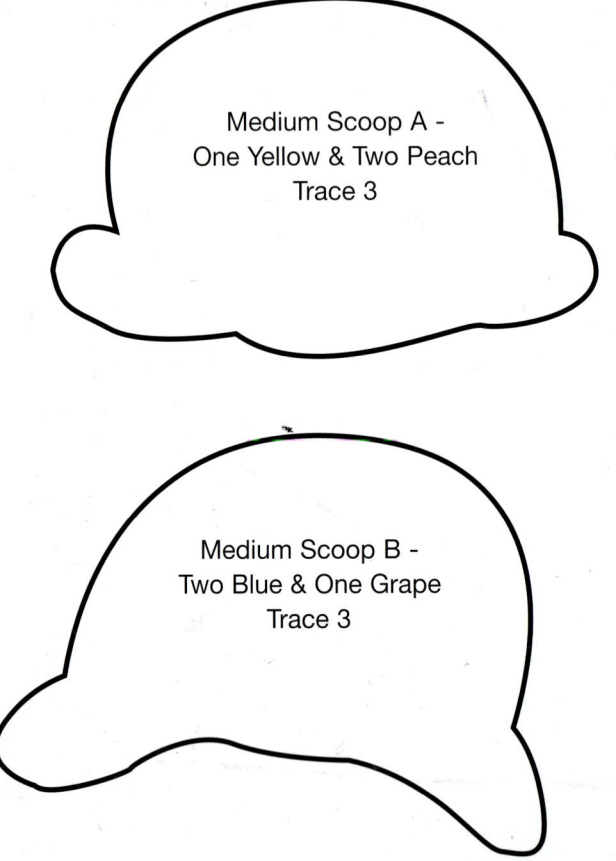

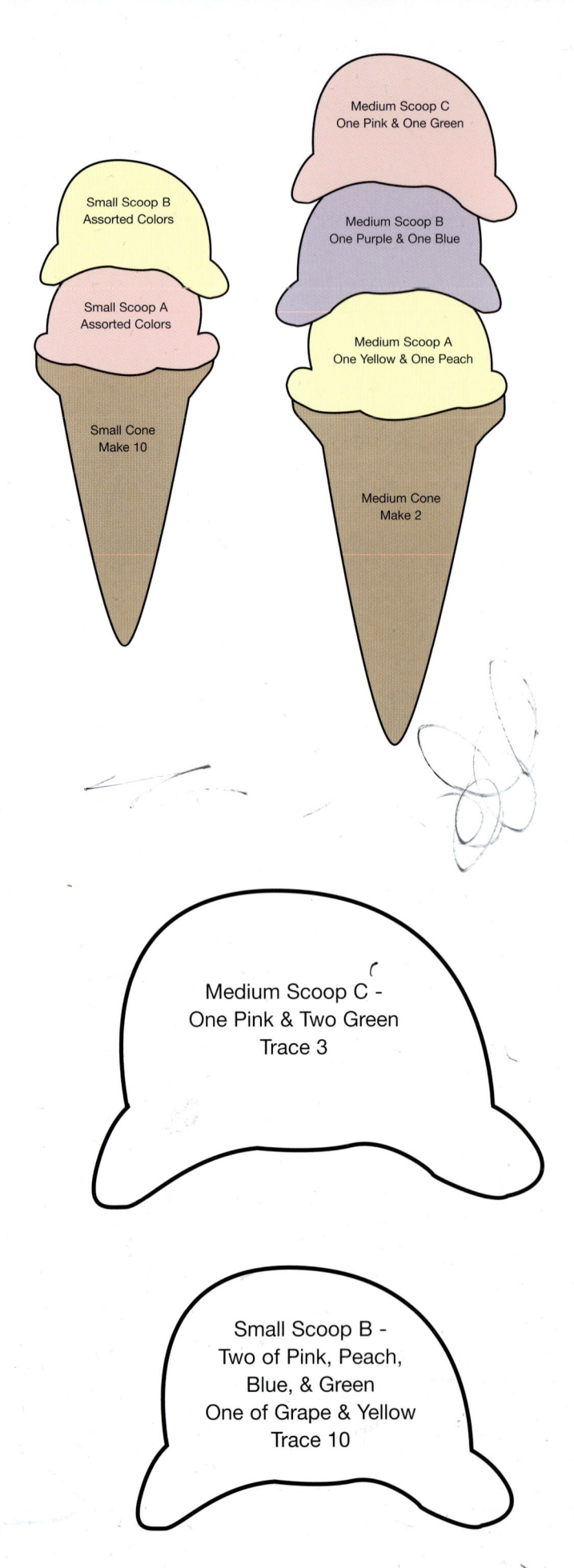

Medium Scoop A -
One Yellow & Two Peach
Trace 3

Medium Scoop C -
One Pink & Two Green
Trace 3

Medium Scoop B -
Two Blue & One Grape
Trace 3

Small Scoop B -
Two of Pink, Peach,
Blue, & Green
One of Grape & Yellow
Trace 10

Medium Hot Fudge - Brown

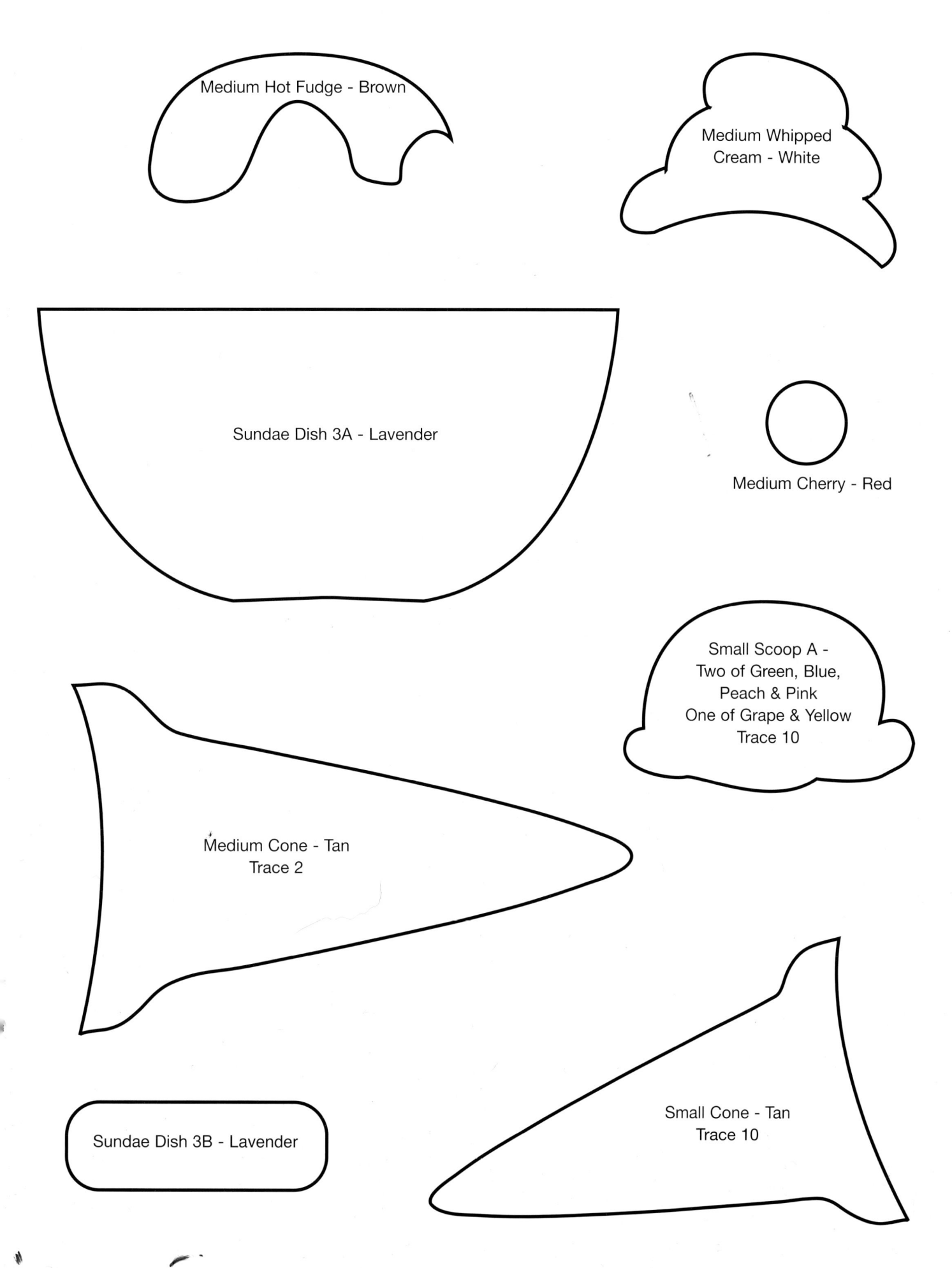

Medium Whipped Cream - White

Sundae Dish 3A - Lavender

Medium Cherry - Red

Small Scoop A -
Two of Green, Blue,
Peach & Pink
One of Grape & Yellow
Trace 10

Medium Cone - Tan
Trace 2

Sundae Dish 3B - Lavender

Small Cone - Tan
Trace 10

Quilt Top Diagram

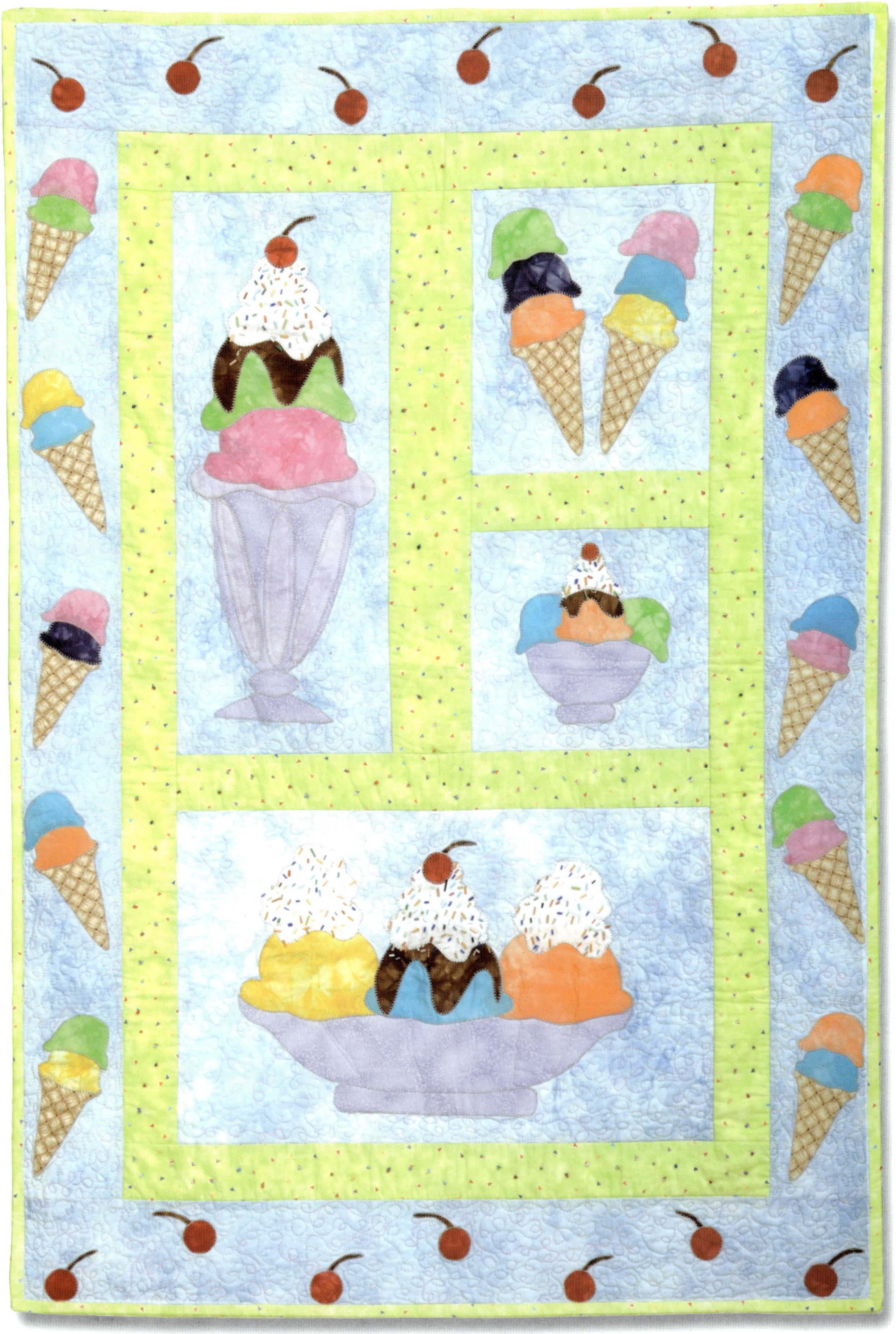

Tweet-Tweet Street

Supplies Needed:

FABRIC:

1/2 yd. (46 cm)	Birdhouse Roof, Stand - Brown
1 3/8 yd. (1.3 m)	Background - Powder Blue
1/2 yd. (46 cm)	Birdhouse Walls, Bird Accents - Yellow
1/2 yd. (46 cm)	Diamond Corners - Lavender Print
1/4 yd. (23 cm)	Checks, Leaves - Dark Green
3/4 yd. (69 cm)	Checks, Middle Border, Flowers, Bird Bellies - Pink
1/4 yd. (23 cm)	Bird Bodies, Flowers - Orange
3/8 yd. (34 cm)	Inner Border, Leaves - Light Green
1 yd. (.91 m)	Stripe Outer Border - Purple
1/2 yd. (46 cm)	Birdhouse Holes, Flower Centers, Binding - Purple
1/8 yd. (11 cm)	Bird Eyeballs - White
1/8 yd. (11 cm)	Bird Eyes - Black
3 1/4 yds. (3 m)	Fabric for Backing

Other Supplies:

2 yds. (1.8 m) Paper-backed Fusible Web
Stabilizer
58" (147 cm) Square of Batting
Appliqué Pressing Sheet
Template Plastic
Black Embroidery Floss

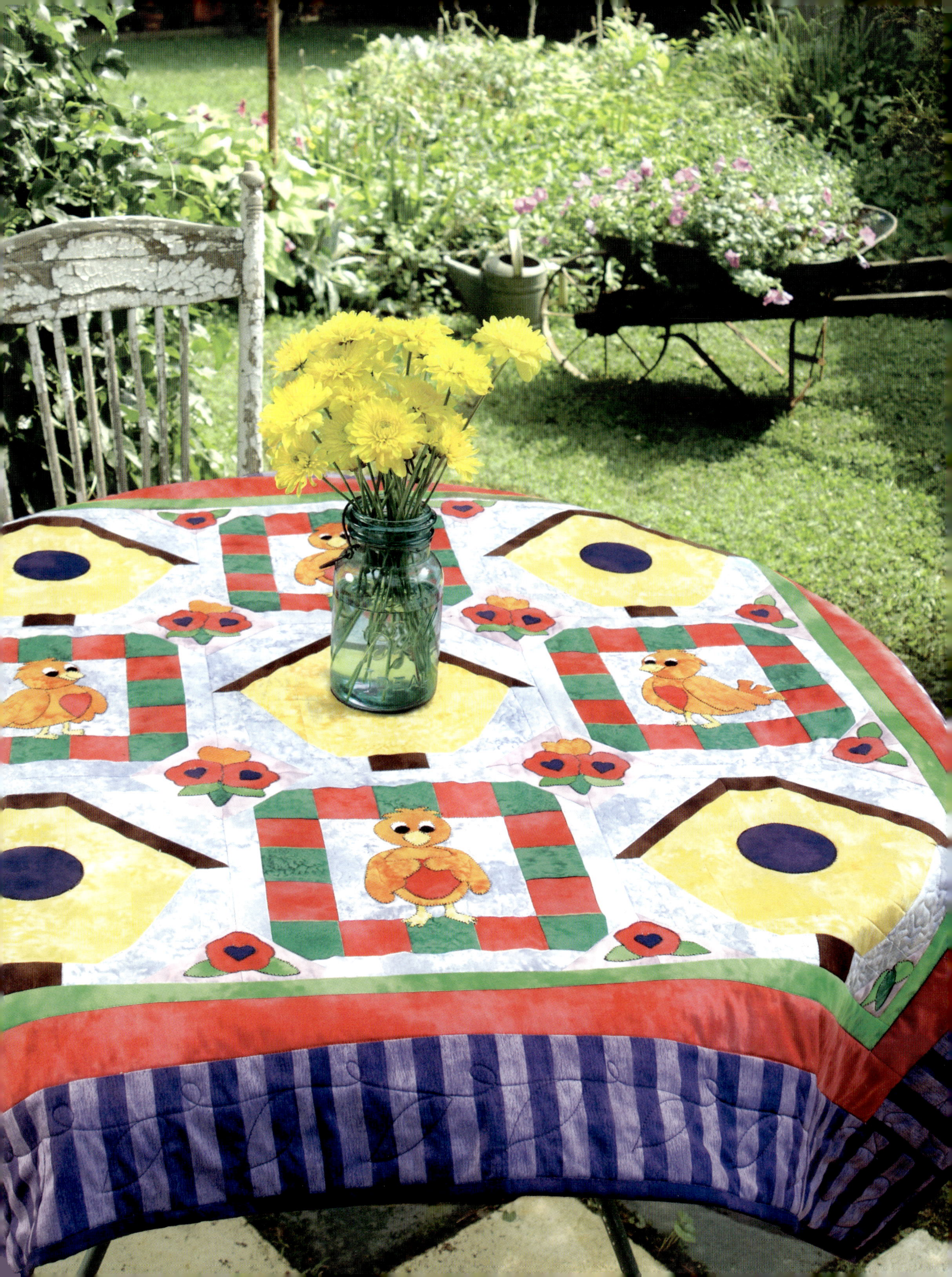

Tweet-Tweet Street

By Heidi Pridemore

Finished Size: 51" x 51"

Pattern Level: Advanced Beginner

All seam allowances are ¼".

Please read all directions before beginning and press carefully step-by-step.

Note: This Pattern has been written to use the fusible web appliqué technique. I recommend using an appliqué pressing sheet for easier assembly.

CUTTING OUT THE PIECES

All measurements include a ¼" seam allowance. Follow **Rotary Cutting**, page 68, to cut fabric. Refer to **Template Cutting**, page 69, to make templates for A and B, page 61. Refer to **Preparing Fusible Appliqués**, page 70, to use patterns, pages 62-65.

From brown fabric, cut:
- Ten 5½" squares
- Ten 1½" x 2½" pieces

From powder blue background fabric, cut:
- Thirteen 1½" x 12½" pieces
- Ten 5½" squares
- Five Template A
- Five Template B
- Ten 1½" x 4½" pieces
- Ten 1½" x 3½" pieces
- Ten 1½" x 5½" pieces
- Eight 1½" x 10½" pieces
- Four 6½" squares
- Ten 1½" squares

From yellow fabric, cut:
- Ten 4½" squares
- Five 2½" x 4½" pieces
- Five 5½" x 6½" pieces
- Five Template A
- Five Template B

From lavender fabric, cut:
- Thirty-six 3½" squares

From dark green fabric, cut
- Thirty-two 2½" squares

From pink fabric, cut:
- Thirty-two 2½" squares
- Two 2½" x 38½" strips
- Two 2½" x 42½" strips, pieced as necessary

From light green fabric, cut:
- Two 1½" x 36½" strips
- Two 1½" x 38½" strips

From the purple striped fabric, cut:
- Five 4½" strips

From purple fabric, cut:
- Six 2¼" strips

To cut out the appliqué pieces:
1. Following the manufacturer's instructions, trace all the bird and flower patterns and the bird house hole on the paper side of the fusible web. Roughly cut out each shape.
2. Fuse the shapes on the back side of the fabric listed on the pattern.
3. Cut out each shape on the traced lines.

MAKING THE BLOCKS

Follow **Piecing and Pressing**, page 69, to make blocks. Refer to **The Sew-and-Flip Technique**, page 77, to make block.

BIRDHOUSE BLOCKS:

1. Place one 5½" powder blue background square on one 5½" brown square, right sides together. Sew one of the diagonals. **(Fig. 1)**

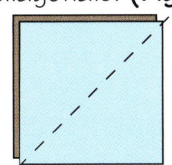

   Fig. 1

2. Trim away the excess fabric, leaving a ¼" seam allowance. **(Fig. 2)** Press open to make a half square triangle. **(Fig. 3)**

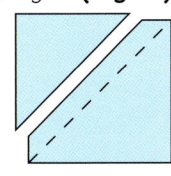

   Fig. 2

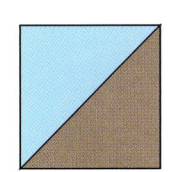

   Fig. 3

3. Place one 4½" yellow square on the brown corner of the half-square triangle. **(Fig. 4)**

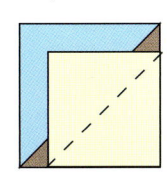

   Fig. 4

4. Sew along the diagonal of the yellow square. Trim away the excess yellow fabric, leaving a ¼" seam allowance **(Fig. 4)**. Press the birdhouse triangle open to form one Unit A. **(Fig. 5)**

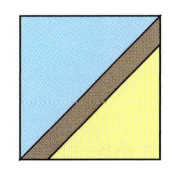

   Fig. 5

   Make ten of Unit A

5. Repeat steps 1 through 4 to make ten Unit As in all.

6. Sew one 1½" x 2½" brown piece to the top of one 2½" x 4½" yellow piece to make one Unit B **(Fig. 6)**. Repeat to make five Unit Bs in all.

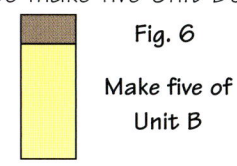

   Fig. 6

   Make five of Unit B

7. Place one powder blue A on one yellow A, right sides together **(Fig. 7)**. (For correct alignment, a ¼" dog ear of each fabric should peek out from the top and bottom.) Sew the two pieces together. Press open to make Unit C. **(Fig. 8)** Make five Unit Cs in all.

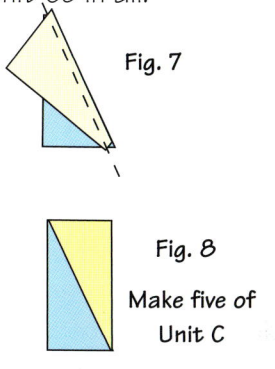

   Fig. 7

   Fig. 8

   Make five of Unit C

8. Place one powder blue B on one yellow B, right sides together. (For correct alignment, a ¼" dog ear of each fabric should peek out from the top and bottom.) Sew the two pieces together. Press open to make Unit D. **(Fig. 9)** Make five Unit Ds in all.

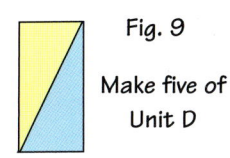

   Fig. 9

   Make five of Unit D

9. Place one 1½" powder blue square on one corner of one 5½" x 6½" yellow piece. Sew along the diagonal **(Fig. 10)**. Trim away the excess powder blue fabric, leaving a ¼" seam allowance.

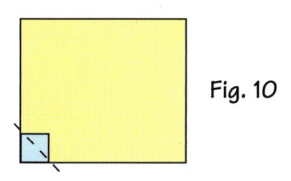

   Fig. 10

10. Place another 1½" powder blue square on the

other bottom corner of the yellow piece **(Fig. 11)**. Sew along the diagonal. Trim away the excess powder blue fabric, leaving a 1/4" seam allowance. This is Unit E. Make five in all.

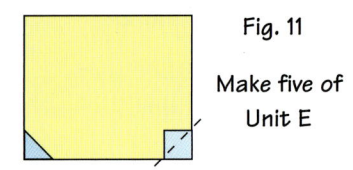

Fig. 11

Make five of Unit E

11. Following the **Birdhouse Block Assembly Diagram**, make five Birdhouse Blocks.

Birdhouse Block Assembly Diagram

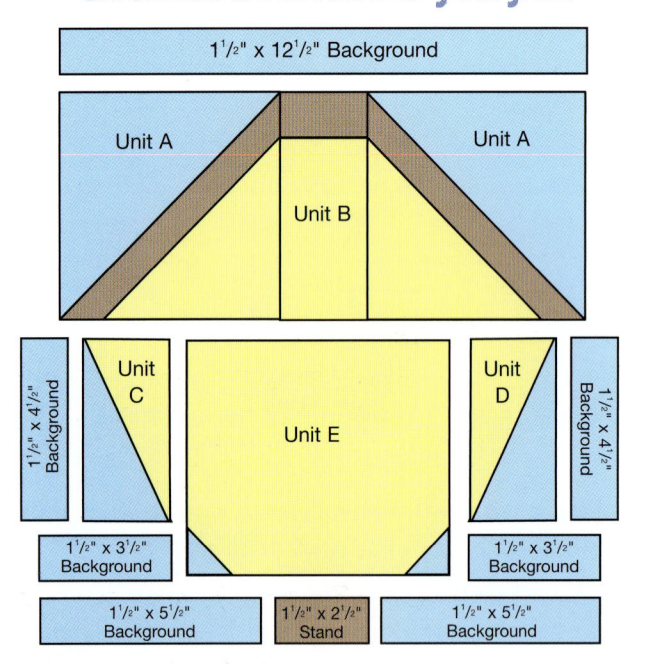

12. Place one 3 1/2" lavender square on one corner of the pieced Birdhouse Block. Sew along the diagonal. Trim away the excess lavender fabric, leaving a 1/4" seam allowance. **(Fig. 12)**

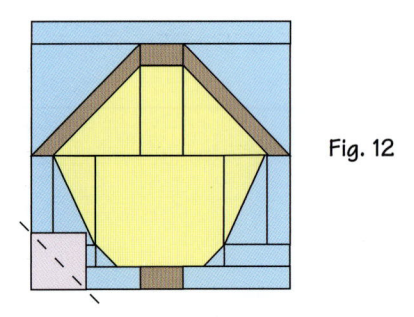

Fig. 12

13. Repeat on the other three corners with 3 1/2" lavender squares. **(Fig. 13)**

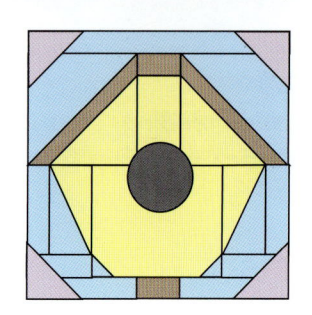

Fig. 13

14. Repeat Steps 12 and 13 to complete the rest of the Birdhouse Blocks. Make five total.

APPLIQUÉS ON BIRDHOUSE BLOCKS:
1. Fuse one birdhouse hole on the center of each birdhouse.
2. Finish the raw edges of each hole with a decorative stitch such as a buttonhole or satin stitch.

BIRD BLOCKS:
1. Sew one 2 1/2" pink square on either side of one 2 1/2" dark green square to make the checked side border strip **(Fig. 14)**. Make eight border strips in all.

Fig. 14

2. Starting with a 2 1/2" dark green square, alternate pink and dark green squares. Sew together three dark green squares and two pink squares to make the top border. **(Fig. 15)** Repeat the sequence to make a bottom border. Repeat to make four top borders and four bottom borders in all.

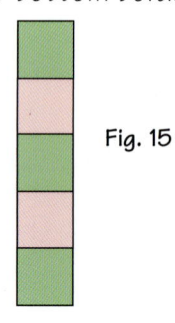

Fig. 15

3. Following the **Bird Block Assembly Diagram**, make four Bird Blocks.
4. Place one 3 1/2" lavender square on one corner of the pieced Bird Block. Sew along the diagonal and

60

trim away the excess lavender fabric, leaving a ¼" seam allowance.
5. Repeat on the other three corners with 3½" lavender squares.
6. Repeat Steps 4 and 5 to complete the rest of the Bird Blocks.

Bird Block Assembly Diagram

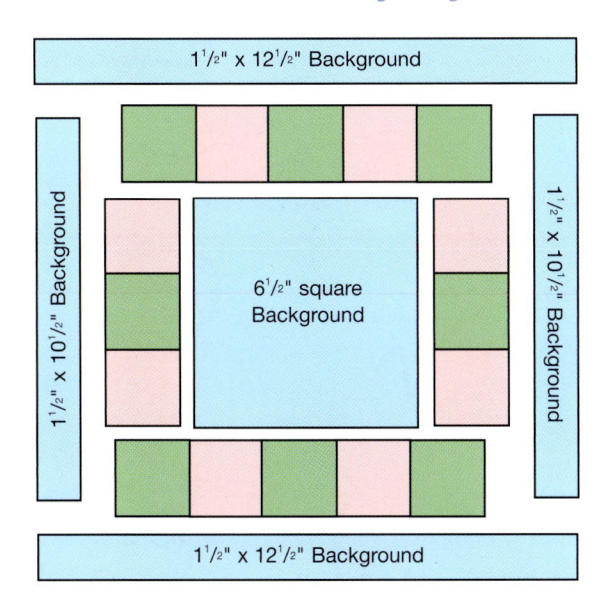

(Diagram shows a 6½" square Background in center, surrounded by pink and green squares, with 1½" x 10½" Background strips on left and right sides, and 1½" x 12½" Background strips on top and bottom.)

TOP ASSEMBLY:
Following the **Quilt Top Diagram**, sew together the Bird Blocks and Birdhouse Blocks to create the quilt top.

BIRD APPLIQUÉS
1. Using an appliqué pressing sheet, assemble the birds. Press and remove from sheet. Fuse one bird in the center of each completed Bird Block. See the **Quilt Top Diagram** as a guide for placement.
2. Finish the raw edges of each bird with a decorative stitch such as a buttonhole or satin stitch. Add beak details with black embroidery floss.

BORDERS:
Use the project photo as a guide.
1. Sew one 1½" x 36½" light green strip to each side of the quilt top.
2. Sew 1½" x 38½" light green strips to the top and bottom of the quilt top.
3. Sew one 2½" x 38½" pink strip to each side of the quilt top.
4. Sew 2½" x 42" pink strips, pieced as necessary, to the top and bottom of the quilt top.
5. Sew one 4½" x 42½" purple striped strip, pieced as necessary, to each side of the quilt top.
6. Piece the remaining purple striped fabric strips to make two 4½" x 50½" strips. Sew them to the top and bottom of the quilt top.

FLOWER APPLIQUÉS:
1. Following the **Quilt Top Diagram**, fuse the flowers and leaves to the quilt top.
2. Finish all the raw edges with decorative stitches, such as a buttonhole or satin stitch.

COMPLETING THE QUILT
1. Follow **Quilting**, page 71, to mark, layer, and quilt as desired.
2. Follow **Making Straight Grain Binding**, page 73, and **Attaching Binding with Mitered Corners**, page 73, to attach binding to quilt.

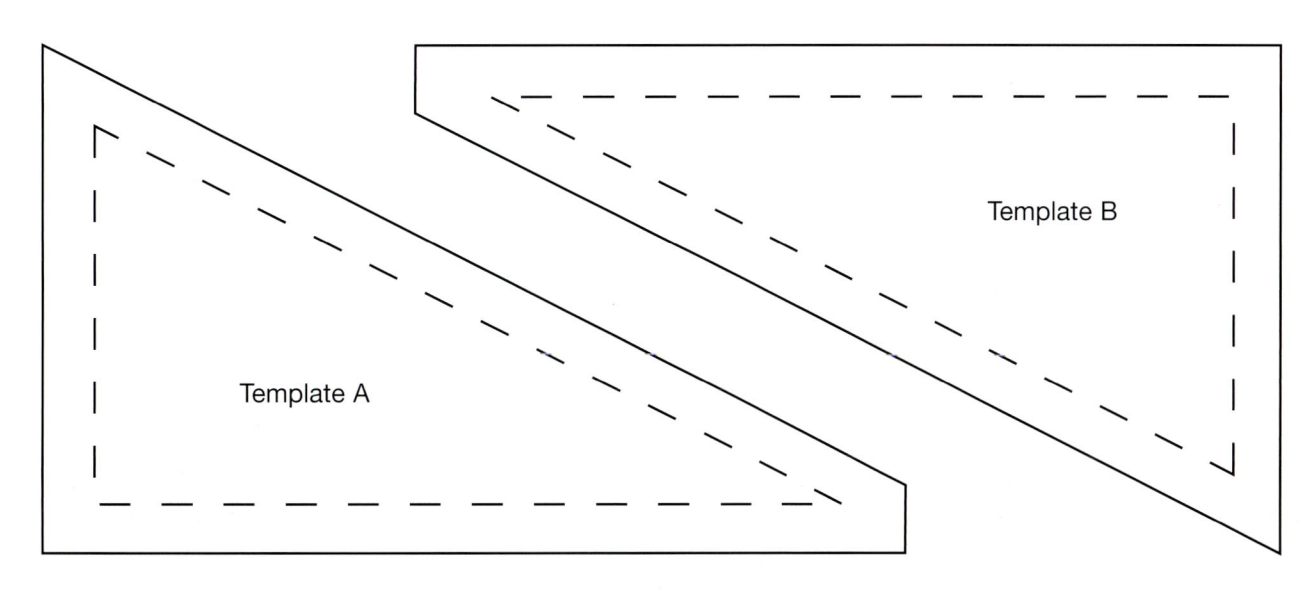

Template A

Template B

Bird A Assembly Drawing

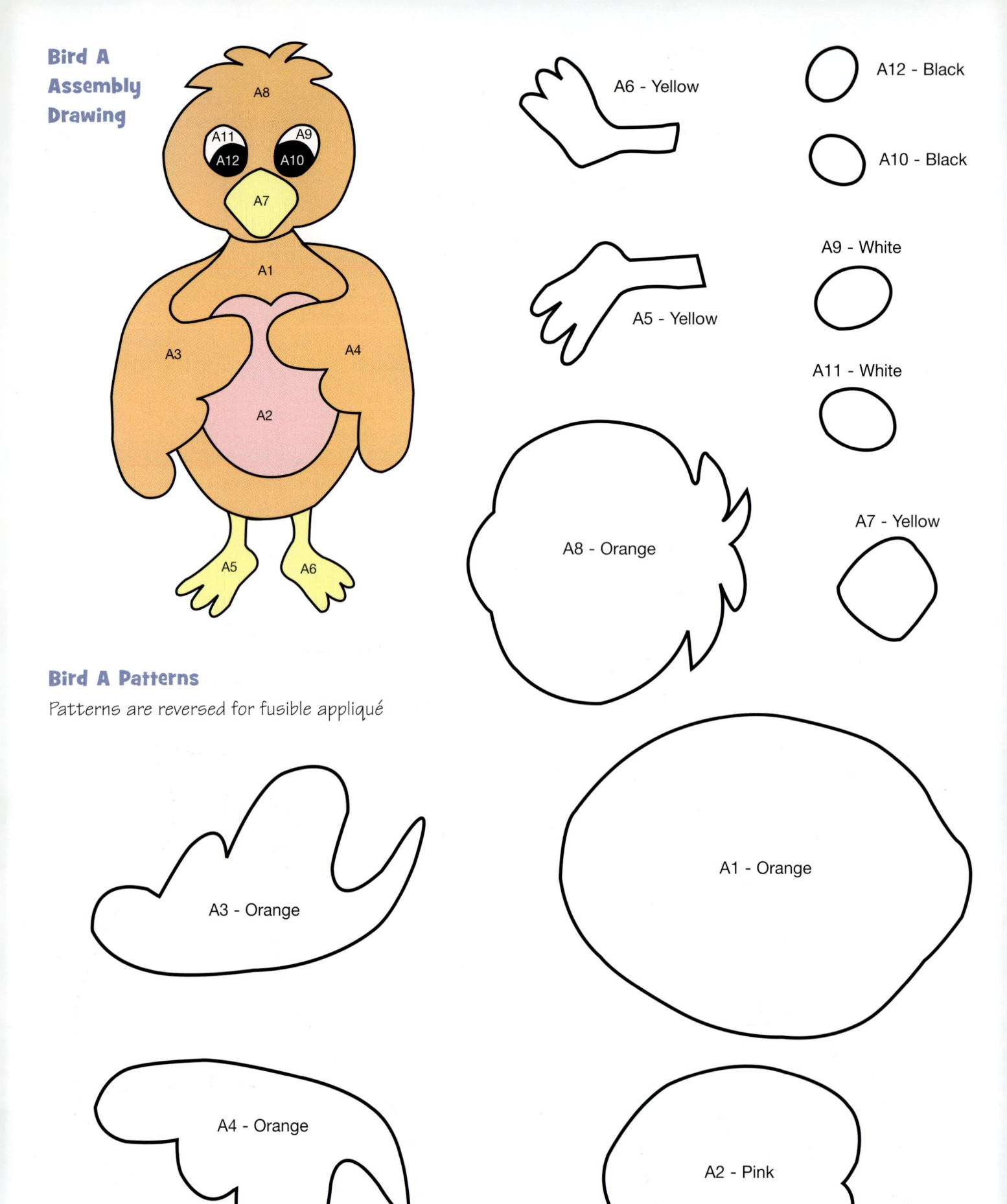

A6 - Yellow

A12 - Black

A10 - Black

A5 - Yellow

A9 - White

A11 - White

A8 - Orange

A7 - Yellow

Bird A Patterns

Patterns are reversed for fusible appliqué

A3 - Orange

A1 - Orange

A4 - Orange

A2 - Pink

Bird B Assembly Drawing

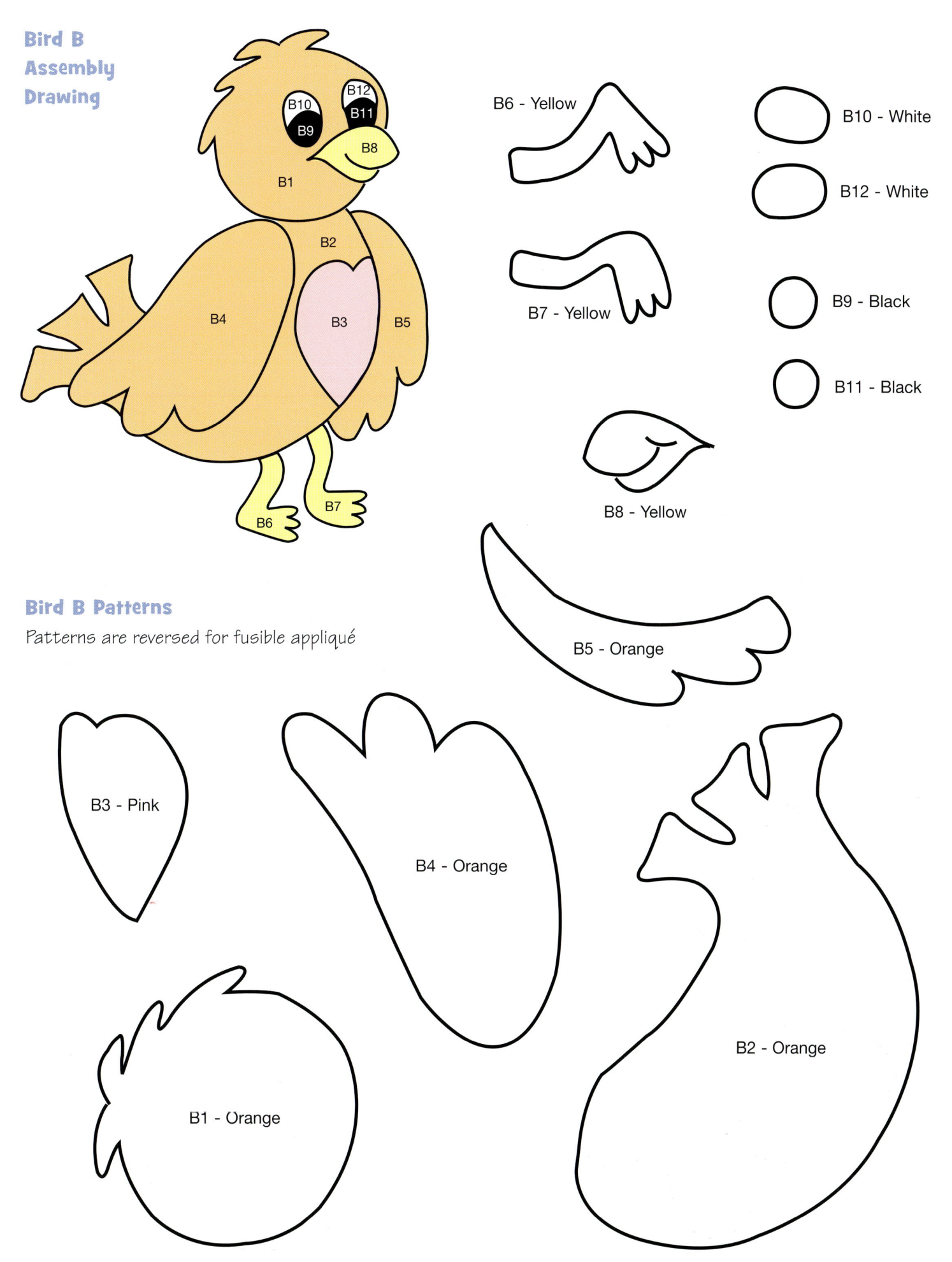

Bird B Patterns

Patterns are reversed for fusible appliqué

B6 - Yellow

B7 - Yellow

B8 - Yellow

B5 - Orange

B10 - White

B12 - White

B9 - Black

B11 - Black

B3 - Pink

B4 - Orange

B1 - Orange

B2 - Orange

Bird C Assembly Drawing

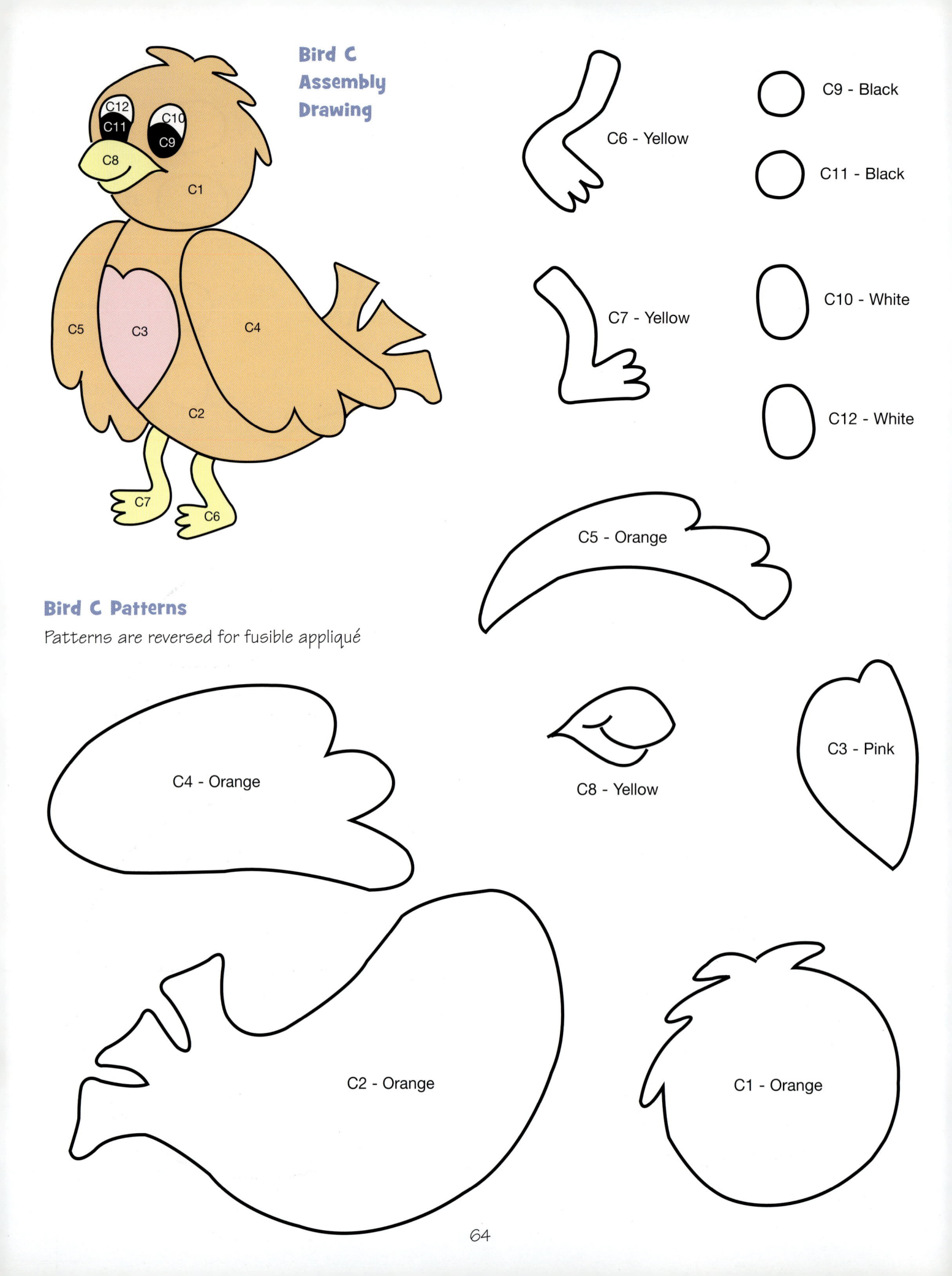

C6 - Yellow
C9 - Black
C11 - Black
C7 - Yellow
C10 - White
C12 - White
C5 - Orange

Bird C Patterns

Patterns are reversed for fusible appliqué

C4 - Orange
C8 - Yellow
C3 - Pink
C2 - Orange
C1 - Orange

Flowers & Leaves Assembly Drawings

Flowers & Leaves Patterns

Patterns are reversed for fusible appliqué

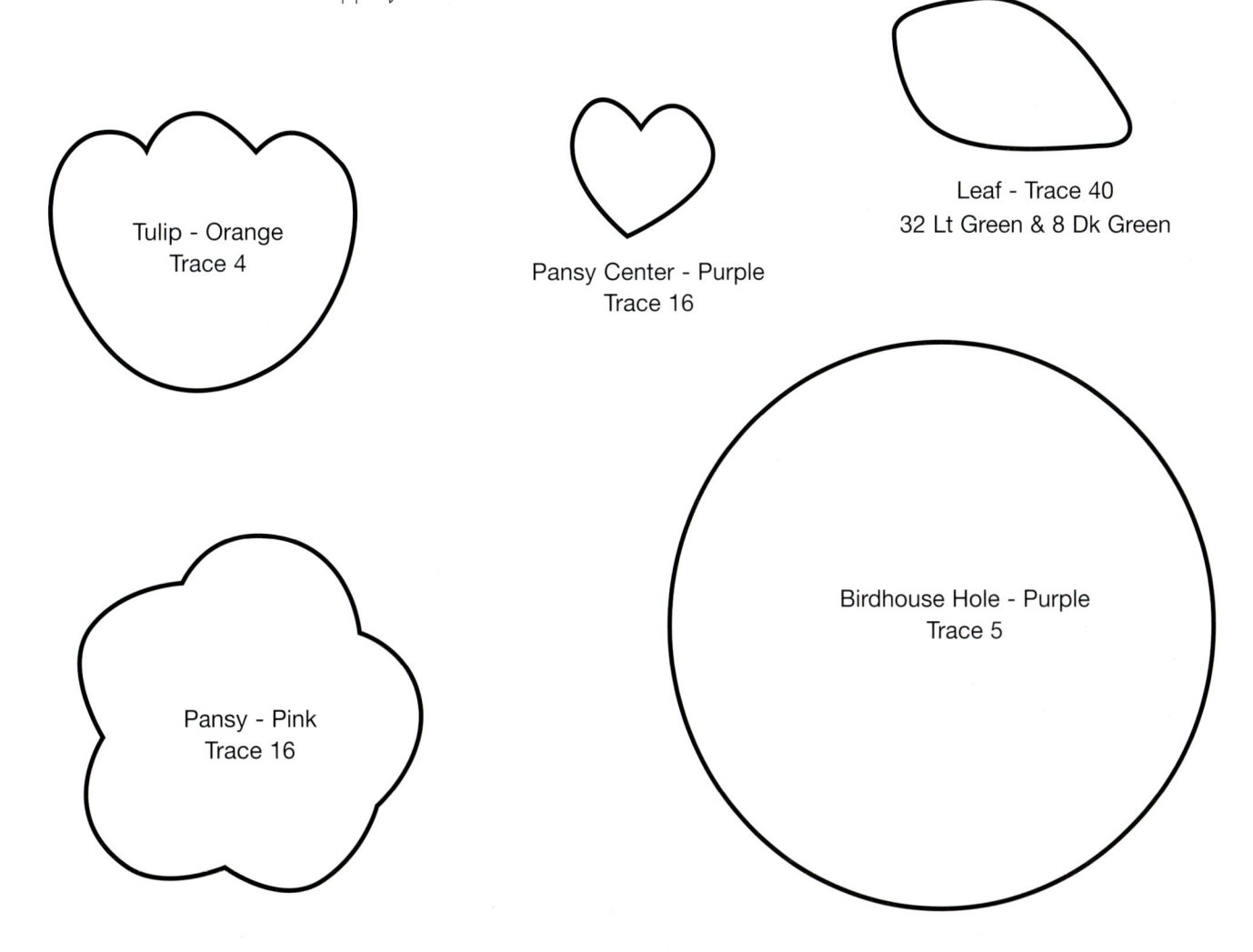

Tulip - Orange
Trace 4

Pansy Center - Purple
Trace 16

Leaf - Trace 40
32 Lt Green & 8 Dk Green

Pansy - Pink
Trace 16

Birdhouse Hole - Purple
Trace 5

Quilt Top Diagram

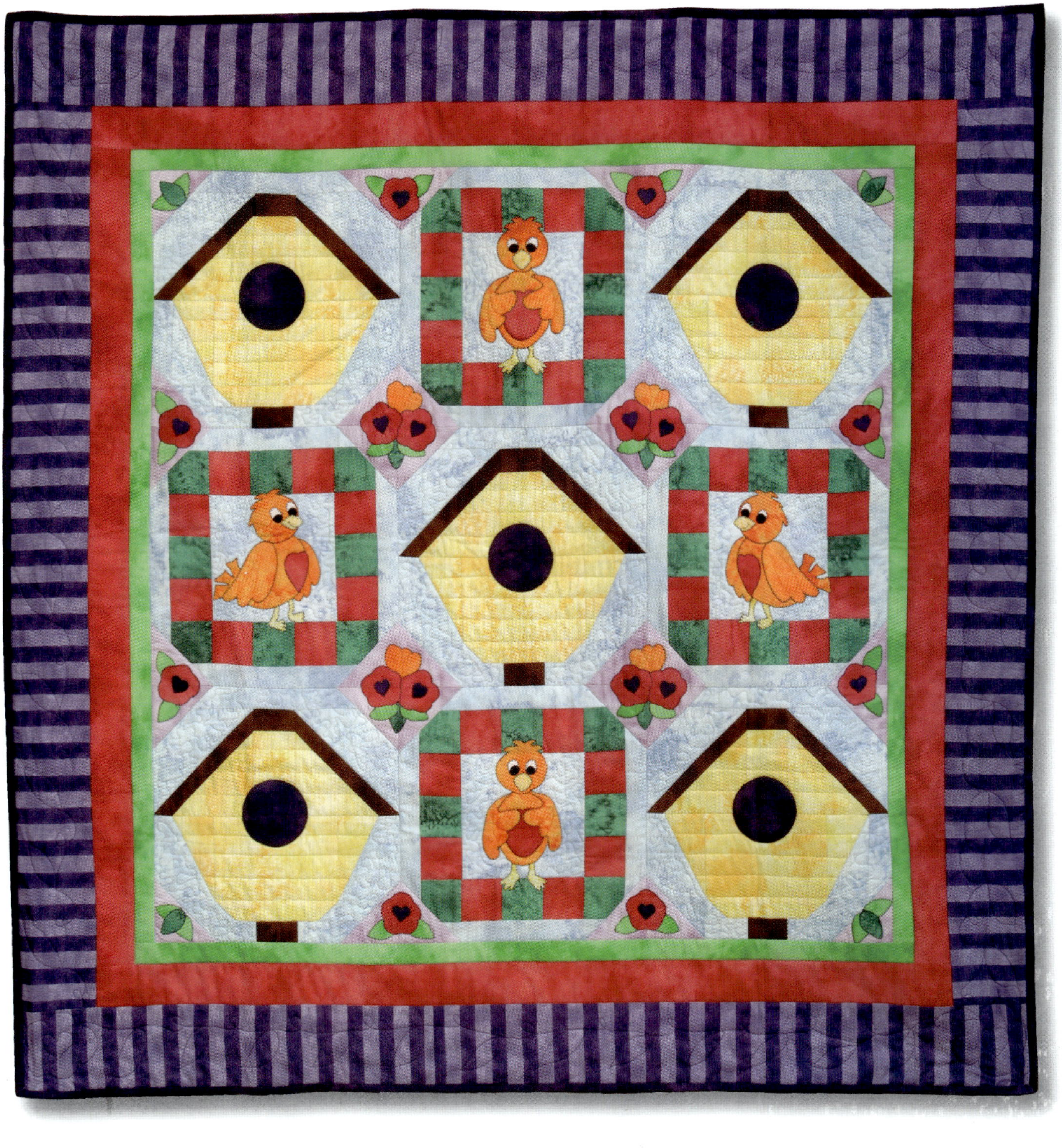

General Instructions

To make your quilting easier and more enjoyable, we encourage you to carefully read all of the general instructions, study the color photographs, and familiarize yourself with the individual project instructions before beginning a project.

FABRICS

SELECTING FABRICS

Choose high-quality, medium-weight 100% cotton fabrics. All-cotton fabrics hold a crease better, fray less, and are easier to quilt than cotton/polyester blends.

Yardage requirements listed for each project are based on 43"/44" wide fabric with a "usable" width of 40" after shrinkage and trimming selvages. Actual usable width will probably vary slightly from fabric to fabric. Our recommended yardage lengths should be adequate for occasional re-squaring of fabric when many cuts are required.

PREPARING FABRICS

We recommend that all cotton fabrics be washed, dried, and pressed before cutting. If fabrics are not pre-washed, washing the finished quilt will cause shrinkage and give it a more "antique" look and feel. Bright and dark colors, which may run, should always be washed before cutting. After washing and drying fabric, fold lengthwise with wrong sides together and matching selvages.

ROTARY CUTTING

Rotary cutting has brought speed and accuracy to quiltmaking by allowing quilters to easily cut strips of fabric and then cut those strips into smaller pieces.

- Place fabric on work surface with fold closest to you.
- Cut all strips from the selvage-to-selvage width of the fabric unless otherwise indicated in project instructions.
- Square left edge of fabric using rotary cutter and rulers **(Figs. 1 - 2)**.
- To cut each strip required for a project, place ruler over cut edge of fabric, aligning desired marking on ruler with cut edge; make cut **(Fig. 3)**.
- When cutting several strips from a single piece of fabric, it is important to make sure that cuts remain at a perfect right angle to the fold; square fabric as needed.

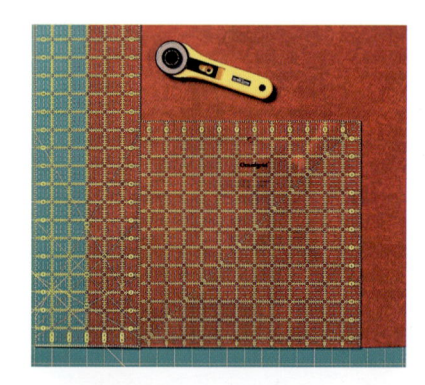

Fig. 1

Fig. 2

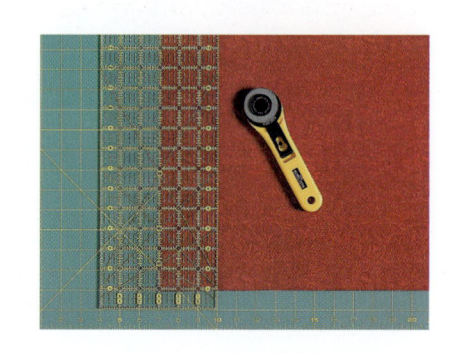

Fig. 3

68

PIECING

Precise cutting, followed by accurate piecing, will ensure that all pieces of the quilt top fit together well.

HAND PIECING

- Use a ruler and a sharp fabric marking pencil to draw all seam lines and transfer any alignment marking onto the back of cut pieces.
- Matching right sides, pin two pieces together, using pins to mark the corners.
- Use a Running Stitch to sew pieces together along drawn line, backstitching at beginning and end of seam.
- Do not extend stitches into seam allowances.
- Run five or six stitches onto the needle before pulling needle through fabric.
- To add stability, backstitch every $3/4$" to 1".

MACHINE PIECING

- Set sewing machine stitch length for approximately 11 stitches per inch.
- Use neutral-colored general-purpose sewing thread (not quilting thread) in the needle and in the bobbin.
- An accurate $1/4$" seam allowance is essential. Presser feet that are $1/4$" wide are available for most sewing machines.
- When piecing, always place pieces right sides together and match raw edges; pin if necessary.
- Chain piecing saves time and will usually result in more accurate piecing.
- Trim away points of seam allowances that extend beyond edges of sewn pieces.

SEWING ACROSS SEAM INTERSECTIONS

When sewing across intersection of two seams, place pieces right sides together and match seams exactly, making sure seam allowances are pressed in opposite directions **(Fig. 4)**.

SEWING SHARP POINTS

To ensure sharp points when joining triangular or diagonal pieces, stitch across the center of the "X" (shown in pink) formed on the wrong side by previous seams **(Fig. 5)**.

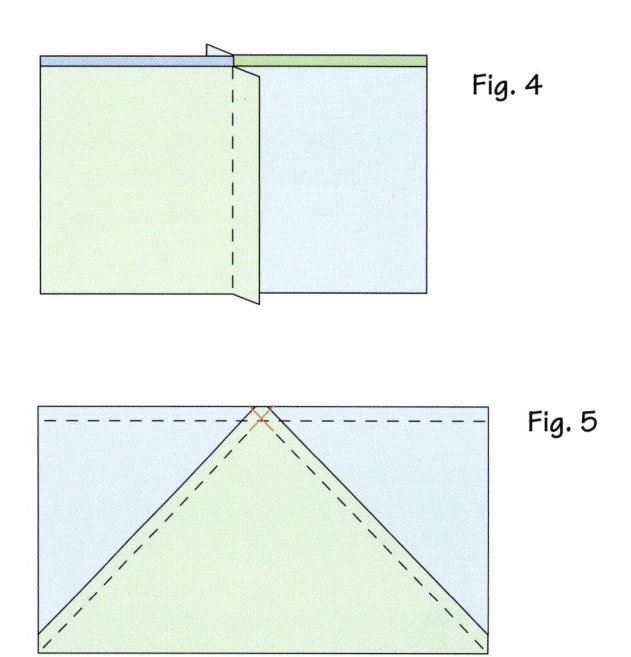

Fig. 4

Fig. 5

PRESSING

- Use a steam iron set on "Cotton" for all pressing.
- Press after sewing each seam.
- Seam allowances are almost always pressed to one side, usually toward the darker fabric. However, to reduce bulk it may occasionally be necessary to press seam allowances toward the lighter fabric or even to press them open.
- To prevent a dark fabric seam allowance from showing through a light fabric, trim the darker seam allowance slightly narrower than the lighter seam allowance.
- To press long seams, such as those in long strip sets, without curving or other distortion, lay strips across the width of the ironing board.

TEMPLATE CUTTING

1. Our piecing template patterns have two lines: a solid cutting line and a dashed line showing the $1/4$" seam allowance. To make a template from a pattern, use a permanent fine-point pen and a ruler to carefully trace pattern onto template plastic, making sure to transfer any alignment (dots) and grainline markings. Cut out template

along inner edge of drawn line. Check template against original pattern for accuracy.
2. Place template face down on wrong side of fabric aligning grainline on template with straight grain of fabric. Use a sharp fabric-marking pencil to draw around template. Transfer all alignment markings (dots) to fabric. Cut out fabric piece along outer drawn lines using scissors or rotary cutting equipment.

APPLIQUÉ
PREPARING FUSIBLE APPLIQUÉ PIECES
White or light-colored fabrics may need to be lined with fusible interfacing before applying fusible web to prevent darker fabrics from showing through.
1. Place paper-backed fusible web, paper side up, over appliqué pattern. Trace pattern onto paper side of web with pencil as many times as indicated in project instructions for a single fabric.
2. Follow manufacturer's instructions to fuse traced patterns to wrong side of fabrics. Do not remove paper backing.
3. Use scissors to cut out appliqué pieces along traced lines. Remove paper backing from all pieces.

SATIN STITCH APPLIQUÉ
A good satin stitch is a thick, smooth, almost solid line of zigzag stitching that covers the exposed raw edges of appliqué pieces. Note: Some machines have decorative stitches, such as Blanket Stitch, which can also be used. Refer to owner's manual to set machine and follow Satin Stitch technique.
1. Pin a stabilizer, such as paper or any of the commercially available products, on the wrong side of background fabric before stitching appliqués in place.
2. Thread sewing machine with general-purpose thread; use general-purpose thread that matches background fabric in bobbin.
3. Set sewing machine for a medium (approximately 1/8") zigzag stitch and a short stitch length. Slightly loosening the top tension may yield a smoother stitch.
4. Begin by stitching two or three stitches in place (drop feed dogs or set stitch length at 0) to anchor thread. Most of the Satin Stitch should be on the appliqué with the right edge of the stitch falling at the outside edge of the appliqué. Stitch over all exposed raw edges of appliqué pieces.
5. (Note: Dots on Figs. 9 – 14 indicate where to leave the needle in the fabric when pivoting.) For outside corners, stitch just past the corner, stopping with the needle in the background fabric **(Fig. 6)**. Raise presser foot. Pivot project, lower presser foot, and stitch adjacent side **(Fig. 7)**.

Fig. 6

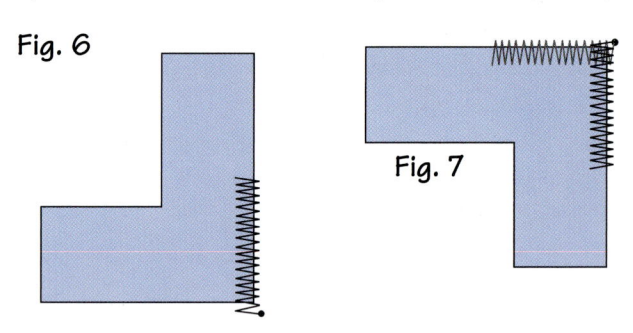

Fig. 7

6. For inside corners, stitch just past the corner, stopping with the needle in the appliqué fabric **(Fig. 8)**. Raise presser foot. Pivot project, lower presser foot, and stitch adjacent side **(Fig. 9)**.

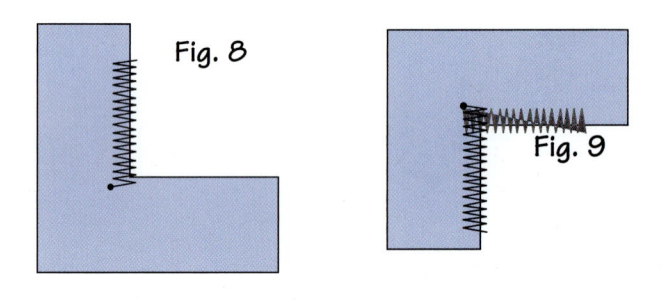

Fig. 8

Fig. 9

7. When stitching outside curves, stop with the needle in the background fabric. Raise presser foot and pivot project as needed. Lower presser foot and continue stitching, pivoting as often as necessary to follow curve **(Fig. 10)**.

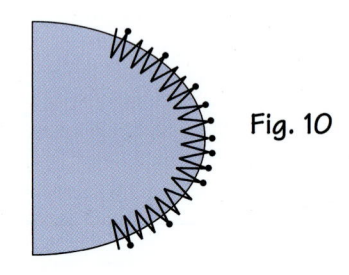

Fig. 10

8. When stitching inside curves, stop with the needle in the appliqué fabric. Raise presser foot and pivot project as needed. Lower presser foot and continue stitching, pivoting as often as necessary to follow curve **(Fig. 11)**.

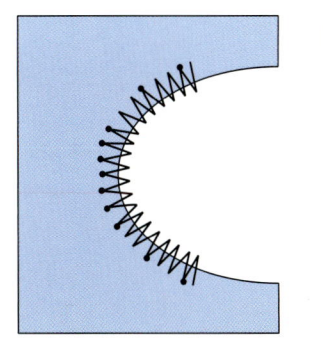

Fig. 11

9. Do not backstitch at the end of stitching. Pull threads to the wrong side of the background fabric; knot thread and trim ends.
10. Carefully tear away stabilizer.

QUILTING

Quilting holds the three layers (top, batting, and backing) of the quilt together and can be done by hand or machine. Because marking, layering, and quilting are interrelated and may be done in different orders depending on circumstances, please read entire Quilting section, pages 71-73, before beginning project.

MARKING QUILTING LINES

Quilting lines may be marked using fabric marking pencils, chalk markers, water, or air-soluble pens, or lead pencils.

Simple quilting designs may be marked with chalk or chalk pencil after basting. A small area may be marked, then quilted, before moving to next area to be marked. Intricate designs should be marked before basting using a more durable marker.

Caution: Some marks may be permanently set by pressing. Test different markers on scrap fabric to find one that marks clearly and can be thoroughly removed.

A wide variety of pre-cut quilting stencils, as well as entire books of quilting patterns, are available. Using a stencil makes it easier to mark intricate or repetitive designs.

To make a stencil from a pattern, center template plastic over pattern and use a permanent marker to trace pattern onto plastic. Use a craft knife with single or double blade to cut channels along traced lines **(Fig. 12)**.

Fig. 12

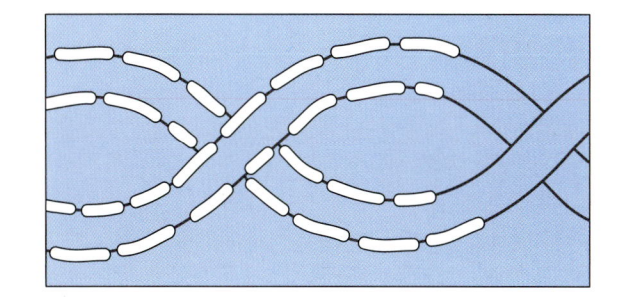

PREPARING THE BACKING

To allow for slight shifting of the quilt top during quilting, backing should be approximately 4" larger on all sides (2" for smaller quilts). Yardage requirements listed for quilt backings are calculated for 43"/44"w fabric with a "useable" width of 40". Using 90"w or 108"w fabric for the backing of a bed-sized quilt may eliminate piecing. To piece a backing using 43"/44"w fabric, use the following instructions.

1. Measure length and width of quilt top; add 8" to each measurement.
2. Cut backing fabric into two lengths slightly longer than determined length measurement. Trim selvages. Place lengths with right sides facing and sew long edges together, forming a tube **(Fig. 13)**. Match seams and press along one fold **(Fig. 14)**. Cut along pressed fold to form a single piece **(Fig. 15)**.

Fig. 13　　Fig. 14　　Fig. 15

3. Trim backing to size determined in Step 1; press seam allowances open.

CHOOSING THE BATTING

The appropriate batting will make quilting easier. For fine hand quilting, choose low-loft batting. All cotton or cotton/polyester blend battings work well for machine quilting because the cotton helps "grip" quilt layers. If a quilt is to be tied, a high-loft batting, sometimes called extra-loft or fat batting, may be used to make the quilt "fluffy."

Types of batting include cotton, polyester, wool, cotton/polyester blend, cotton/wool blend, and silk.

When selecting the batting, refer to package labels for characteristics and care instructions. The batting should be the same size as prepared backing.

ASSEMBLING THE QUILT

1. Examine the wrong side of the quilt top closely; trim any seam allowances and clip any threads that may show through the front of the quilt. Press the quilt top, being careful not to "set" any marked quilting lines.
2. Place backing wrong side up on flat surface. Use masking tape to tape edges of backing to surface. Place batting on top of backing fabric. Smooth batting gently, being careful not to stretch or tear. Center quilt top right side up on batting.
3. If hand quilting, begin in center and work toward outer edges to hand baste all layers together. Use long stitches and place basting lines approximately 4" apart **(Fig. 16)**. Smooth fullness or wrinkles toward outer edges.

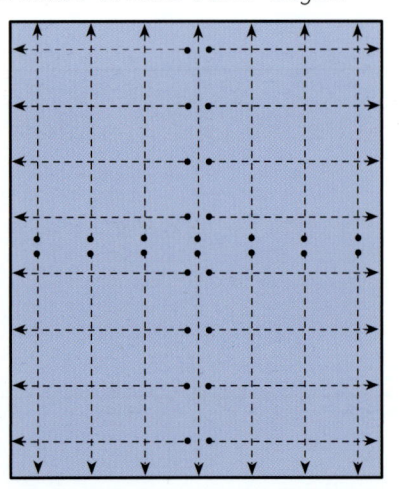

Fig. 16

4. If machine quilting, use 1" rustproof safety pins to "pin-baste" all layers together, spacing pins approximately 4" apart. Begin at center and work toward outer edges to secure all layers. If possible, place pins away from areas that will be quilted, although pins may be removed as needed when quilting.

MACHINE QUILTING METHODS

Use general-purpose thread in the bobbin. Do not use quilting thread. Thread the needle of machine with general-purpose thread or transparent monofilament thread to make quilting blend with quilt top fabrics. Use decorative thread, such as a metallic or contrasting-color general-purpose thread, to make quilting lines stand out more.

Straight Line Quilting:

The term "straight-line" is somewhat deceptive, since curves (especially gentle ones) as well as straight lines can be stitched with this technique.
1. Set stitch length for six to ten stitches per inch and attach a walking foot to sewing machine.
2. Determine which section of the quilt will have the longest continuous quilting line, oftentimes the area from the center top to the center bottom. Roll up and secure each edge of quilt to help reduce the bulk, keeping fabrics smooth. Smaller projects may not need to be rolled.
3. Begin stitching on longest quilting line, using very short stitches for the first $1/4$" to "lock" quilting. Stitch across project, using one hand on each side of walking foot to slightly spread fabric and to guide fabric through machine. Lock stitches at end of quilting line.
4. Continue machine quilting, stitching longer quilting lines first to stabilize quilt before moving onto other areas.

Free Motion Quilting:

Free motion quilting may be free form or may follow a marked pattern.
1. Attach a darning foot to the sewing machine and lower or cover feed dogs.
2. Position quilt under darning foot; lower foot.

Holding top thread, take a stitch and pull bobbin thread to top of quilt. To "lock" beginning of quiling line, hold top and bobbin threads while making three to five stitches in place.

3. Use one hand on each side of darning foot to slightly spread fabric and to move fabric through the machine. Even stitch length is achieved by using smooth, flowing hand motion and steady machine speed. Slow machine speed and fast hand movement will create long stitches. Fast machine speed and slow hand movement will create short stitches. Move quilt sideways, back and forth, in a circular motion, or in a random motion to create desired designs; do not rotate quilt. Lock stitches at end of each quilting line.

BINDING

Binding encloses the raw edges of quilt. Because of its stretchiness, bias binding works well for binding projects with curves or rounded corners and tends to lie smooth and flat in any given circumstance. Binding may also be cut from straight lengthwise or crosswise grain of fabric.

MAKING STRAIGHT-GRAIN BINDING

1. Cut crosswise strips of binding fabric the determined length and the width called for in project instructions. Strips may be pieced to achieve necessary length.
2. Matching wrong sides and raw edges, press strip in half lengthwise to complete binding.

ATTACHING BINDING WITH MITERED CORNERS

1. Beginning with one end near center on bottom edge of quilt, lay binding around quilt to make sure that seams in binding will not end up at a corner. Adjust placement if necessary. Matching raw edges of binding to raw edge of quilt top, pin binding to right side of quilt along one edge.
2. When you reach first corner, mark $1/4$" from the corner of quilt top (Fig. 17).
3. Beginning approximately 10" from end of binding and using $1/4$" seam allowance, sew binding to quilt, backstitching at beginning of stitching and at mark (Fig. 18). Lift needle out of fabric and clip thread.

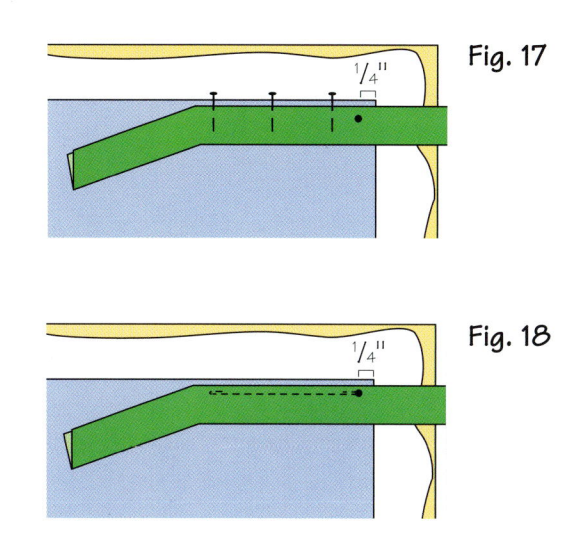

Fig. 17

Fig. 18

4. Fold binding (Figs. 19 – 20) and pin binding to adjacent side, matching raw edges. When you've reached the next corner, mark $1/4$" from the edge of quilt top.

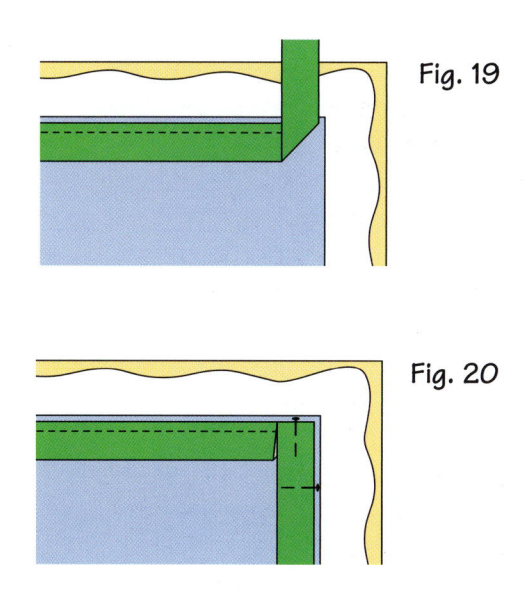

Fig. 19

Fig. 20

5. Backstitching at edge of quilt top, sew pinned binding to quilt (Fig. 21); backstitch at the next mark. Lift needle out of fabric and clip thread.

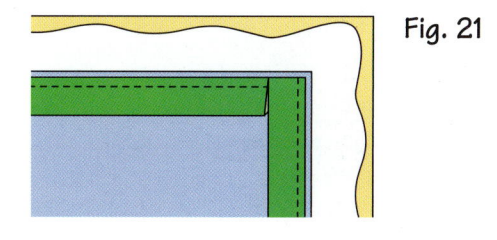

Fig. 21

6. Continue sewing binding to quilt, stopping approximately 10" from starting point (**Fig. 22**).

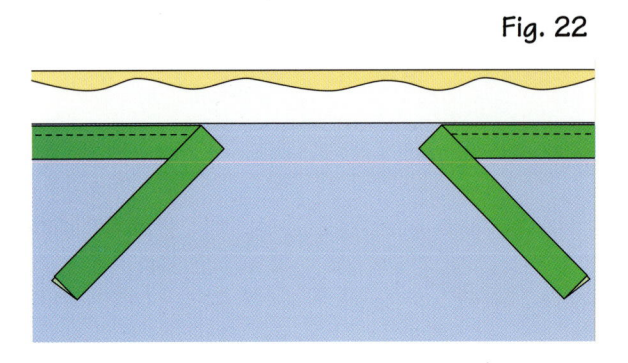

Fig. 22

7. Bring beginning and end of binding to center of opening and fold each end back, leaving a ¼" space between folds (**Fig. 23**). Finger-press folds.

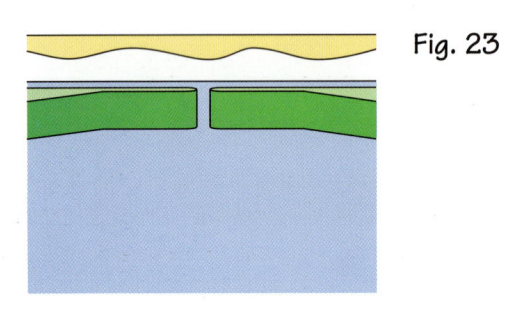

Fig. 23

8. Unfold ends of binding and draw a line across wrong side in finger-pressed crease. Draw a line through the lengthwise pressed fold of binding at same spot to create a cross mark. With edge of ruler at cross mark, line up 45° angle marking on ruler with one long side of binding. Draw a diagonal line from edge to edge. Repeat on remaining end, making sure that the two diagonal lines are angled the same way (**Fig. 24**).

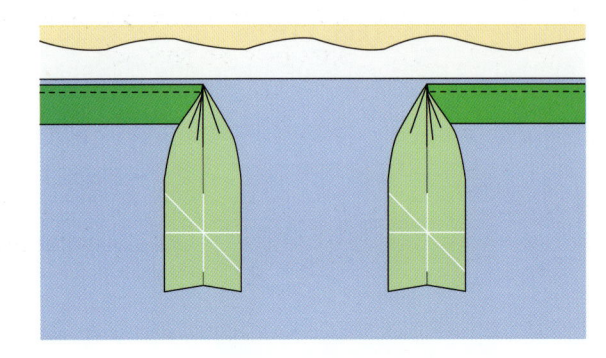

Fig. 24

9. Matching right sides and diagonal lines, pin binding ends together at right angles (**Fig. 25**).

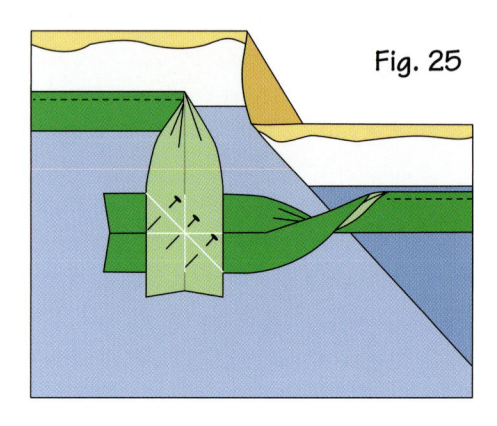

Fig. 25

10. Machine stitch along diagonal line, removing pins as you stitch (**Fig. 26**).

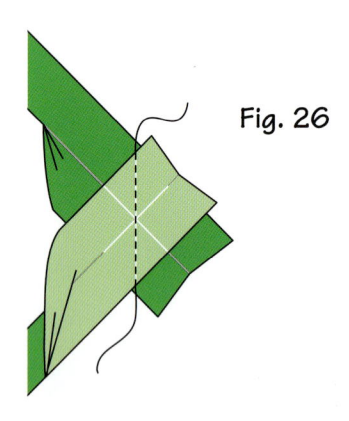

Fig. 26

11. Lay binding against quilt to double-check that it is correct length.
12. Trim binding ends, leaving ¼" seam allowance; press seam open. Stitch binding to quilt.
13. Trim backing and batting a scant ¼" larger than quilt top so that batting and backing will fill the binding when it is folded over to quilt backing.
14. On one edge of quilt, fold binding over to quilt backing and pin pressed edge in place, covering stitching line (**Fig. 27**). On adjacent side, fold binding over, forming a mitered corner (**Fig. 28**). Repeat to pin remainder of binding in place.

Fig. 27

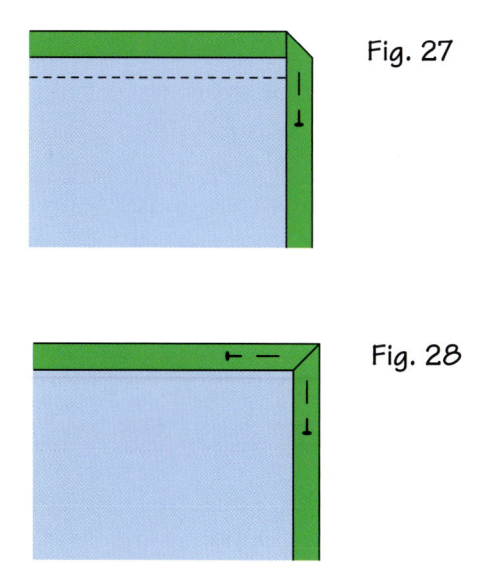

Fig. 28

15. Blindstitch binding to backing, taking care not to stitch through to front of quilt.

BLIND STITCH

Come up at 1, go down at 2, and come up at 3 (**Fig. 29**). Length of stitches may be varied as desired

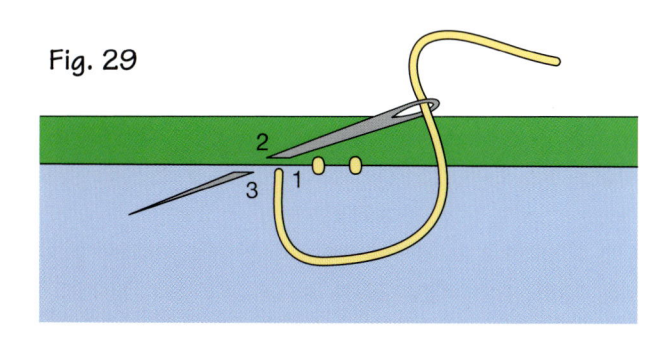

Fig. 29

MAKING CONTINUOUS BIAS STRIP BINDING

Bias strips for binding can simply be cut and pieced to desired length. However, when a long length of binding is needed, the "continuous" method is quick and accurate.
1. Cut square from binding fabric the size indicated in project instructions. Cut square in half diagonally to make two triangles.
2. With right sides together and using a ¼" seam allowance, sew triangles together (**Fig. 30**); press seam allowances open.

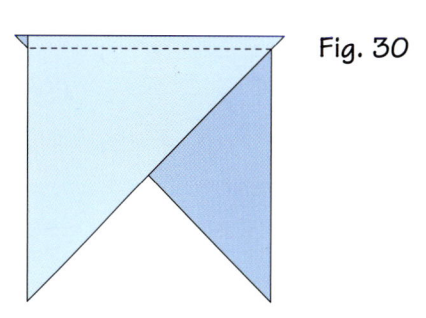

Fig. 30

3. On wrong side of fabric, draw lines the width of binding as specified in project instructions, usually 2½" (**Fig. 31**). Cut off any remaining fabric less than this width.

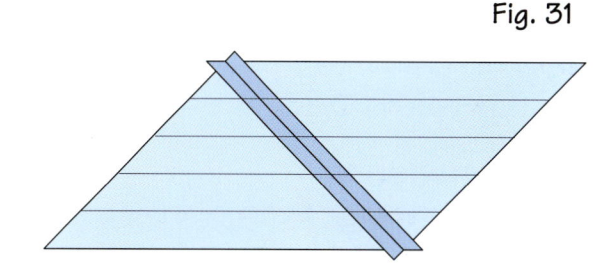

Fig. 31

4. With right sides inside, bring short edges together to form tube; match raw edges so that first drawn line of top section meets second drawn line of bottom section (**Fig. 32**).

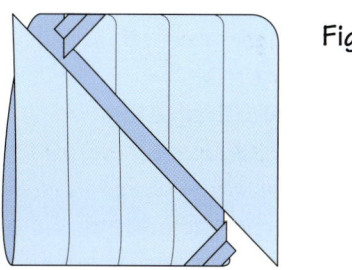

Fig. 32

5. Carefully pin edges together by inserting pins through drawn lines at point where drawn lines intersect, making sure pins go through intersections on both sides. Using ¼" seam allowance, sew edges together; press seam allowances open.
6. To cut continuous strip, begin cutting along first drawn line (**Fig. 33**). Continue cutting along drawn line around tube.

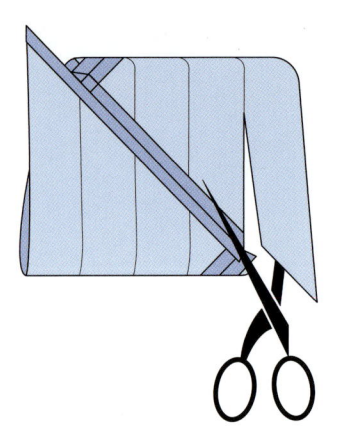

Fig. 33

7. Trim ends of bias strip square.
8. Matching wrong sides and raw edges, carefully press bias strip in half lengthwise to complete binding.

BEADING TECHNIQUES

Here are three beading techniques. Use any or all of them to add "sprinkles" to the ice cream cones and sundaes on this quilt.
- Use a thin needle that will easily pass through the hole of the smallest bead. Thread the needle with hand quilting or polyester thread. Tie a small knot at the end of the thread.
- If the beads are clear, use a thread that matches the bead color. If the beads are opaque, use a thread that matches the background.

SCATTERED BEAD TECHNIQUE:

Use this technique to add beads that are not right next to each other.
1. Stitch through the top layer of the quilt where you want to place the first bead. Pull the thread through until the knot pops through the quilt, stopping at the top layer and catching on the back side. (This is called burying the knot.)
2. Take a small stitch through the quilt top to secure the thread.
3. Thread the bead onto the needle and go through the background a second time.
4. Bring the needle up through the background where you would like your second bead to be. (This can be up to 1" to 2" away.) Travel with your needle between the top and batting layers. Repeat this technique until all the scattered beads are in place or you run short of thread.
5. To tie off the thread, go through the last bead one more time, go through the background, and bring the needle up about an inch away. Tie off the thread and go back through the same hole you came up to bury the knot.

BEADS IN A ROW TECHNIQUE:

Use this technique to add beads that are right next to each other.
1. Stitch through the top layer of the quilt where you want to place the first bead. Pull the thread through until the knot pops through the top layer and catches on the back side.
2. Take a small stitch through the top to secure the thread.
3. Thread the bead on the needle and go through the background a second time.
4. Bring the needle up about $1/16$" away from the first bead. Thread a second bead on the needle, Bring the bead down to the quilt top. Go through the background between the first and second bead. Come back up through the background $1/16$" away from the second bead.
5. Repeat this technique until all the beads are in place or you run short of thread.
6. To tie off the thread, go through the last bead one more time, go through the background, and bring the needle up about an inch away. Tie off the thread and go back through the same hole you came up to bury the knot.

GARLAND BEADS TECHNIQUE:

Use this technique to add beads that drape and hang loose from the top.
1. Use a thin needle that will easily pass through the hole on the smallest bead. Thread it with hand quilting or polyester thread. If the beads are clear use a thread that matches the bead color, or if the beads are opaque use a thread that matches the background you are beading on. Tie a small knot at the end of the thread.
2. Once you have your needle and thread ready, stitch through the top layer of the quilt where

you want to place the first bead. Pull the thread through until the knot pops through the top layer and catches on the back side.
3. Take a small stitch through the top to secure the thread. Now thread a number of beads onto the thread to create the garland. Once you have the length you desire, make a backstitch in the background where the drape looks best. Now thread the bead onto the needle and go through the background a second time.
4. To tie off the thread. Go through the last bead one extra time. Go through the background and bring the needle up about an inch away. Tie off the thread and go back through the same hole you came up to bury the knot.

THE SEW-AND-FLIP TECHNIQUE

The flip-and-sew technique involves placing a smaller square on a larger square or rectangle and sewing from corner to corner of the smaller square. Instead of marking each square on the diagonal, it is easier to use a tool called an Angler or to mark the needle line on your machine.

To make a needle line, raise the presser foot and lower the needle to the down position. Place a ruler on the throat plate of your machine, gently resting it against the needle. Lower the presser foot, making sure the edge of the ruler is exactly parallel to the needle. Place a piece of masking tape on the flatbed of the machine right along the edge of the ruler. Remove the ruler--you will have a straight line from your needle to the front of your machine.

This tape is your guide for the diagonals. Align the top corner of the smaller square you want to sew under your needle. Align the opposite corner on the tape line. Make sure the opposite corner of the smaller square stays on the tape line as you sew the squares together **(Fig. 34)**.

Once the pieces are sewn together, press open the smaller square to form a triangle. You will have three layers of fabric in the corner. Cut the back two layers 1/4" away from the seam. You should now have a larger piece with a smaller triangle in one corner **(Fig. 35)**.

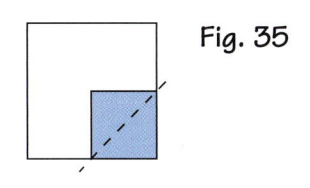

Metric Conversion Chart

Metric Conversions

Inches x 2.54 = centimeters (cm)
Inches x 25.4 = millimeters (mm)
Inches x .0254 = meters (m)

Yards x .9144 = meters (m)
Yards x 91.44 = centimeters (cm)
Centimeters x .3937 = Inches (")
Meters x 1.0936 = yards (yd)

Standard Equivalents

1/8"	3.2 mm	0.32 cm	1/8 yd	11.43 cm	0.11 m
1/4"	6.35 mm	0.635 cm	1/4 yd	22.86 cm	0.23 m
3/8"	9.5 mm	0.95 cm	3/8 yd	34.29 cm	0.34 m
1/2"	12.7 mm	1.27 cm	1/2 yd	45.72 cm	0.46 m
5/8"	15.9 mm	1.59 cm	5/8 yd	57.15 cm	0.57 m
3/4"	19.1 mm	1.91 cm	3/4 yd	68.58 cm	0.69 m
7/8"	22.2 mm	2.22 cm	7/8 yd	80 cm	0.8 m
1"	25.4 mm	2.54 cm	1 yd	91.44 cm	0.91 m

© 2005 by Leisure Arts, Inc., 5701 Ranch Drive, Little Rock, AR 72223. All rights reserved. This publication is protected under federal copyright laws. Reproduction or distribution of this publication or any other Leisure Arts publication, including publications which are out of print, is prohibited unless specifically authorized. This includes, but is not limited to, any form of reproduction or distribution on or through the Internet, including posting, scanning, or e-mail transmission.

We have made every effort to ensure that these instructions are accurate and complete. We cannot, however, be responsible for human error, typographical mistakes, or variations in individual work.

Production Team:
Joel Tressler - Creative Director
Allyson Frye - Graphic Designer
Phyllis Mueller - Technical Writer
April Stephens - Photo Assistant